A New Theory of Music:

An Introduction

H. K. Grumbein

CONTENTS

FOUNDATIONS

The Art of Music

Music is mysterious. It is very difficult to define in objective terms. Music is something like a form of art that works within the medium of sound. That is not to say that music is merely the sounds of the music, because it is also, just as importantly, the silences. It would be more accurate to suggest that music emerges from silence or that music somehow shapes silence. Silence is always around us to the degree that we allow its presence into our lives, but it is never experienced in an absolute way or in its purest form because sound is everywhere that we are. Silence is more than our experience of a mere lack of sound, just as music is more than our experience of the mere presence of sound. Music may be thought of as the creative reconciliation of sound and silence. This is not to imply that either is necessary for something to be music; it is possible for music to have either no silence or no sound at all. However, without silence as a ground or field upon which the sound might be positioned, there cannot be music. Similarly, without the possibility of sound (and often, the sounds that are always around us) there can be no possible experience of music.

Silence can act as a bridge between worlds: it can take us as we are, in our own world, and bring us into contact with something greater. This might be thought of as a higher state of consciousness, or perhaps the experience of our essential or spiritual nature, or maybe even the operation of grace in our lives. In many spiritual and religious traditions, silence is a rudimentary practise within the context of prayer, contemplation, and meditation.

Sound has the ability to cross apparent sensory boundaries because it also has important tactile and visual qualities. Evelyn Glennie is a master musician and virtuoso percussionist despite being profoundly deaf because she set herself to thoroughly explore the feelings of sound in the body. Patrick Flannagan invented a device called the Neurophone which is supposed to allow a person to hear music through the skin. The oscilloscope has allowed scientists to study the visual representations of sound waves travelling through the air. The harmonograph has revealed that geometric shapes can be derived from sound waves. Cymatics is a field of scientific research in which sound waves cause vibrations in membranes covered with various powders or liquids; these vibrations reveal geometric shapes and movements not unlike the magnetic flow lines in iron filings. Hans Jenny was an important pioneer in this field and extensively documented his experiments with lycopodium powder. Many others have experimented with similar phenomena, including Leonardo da Vinci,

Galileo Galilei, and Ernst Chladni. There is an even more bizarre phenomenon known as synaesthesia, which is sometimes related to hearing. In auditory synaesthesia, the auditory signals from hearing a sound cross paths in the brain with other senses, resulting in an accompanying experience of seeing, feeling, tasting and/or smelling of a sound. Many composers have been known to have intense synaesthetic experiences and have used them as an integral part of musical composition; a few examples are Olivier Messiaen, Alexander Scriabin, Franz Liszt, and Nikolai Rimsky-Korsakov.

Another element of music is its organization which unfolds in time. In this way, music is more of a process or activity than something static; and as such, music relies on the passing of time. Time is a fundamental requirement for the experience of sound, whereas silence has no actual reference to time. On the other hand, moments of creativity and inspiration have a distinctively timeless quality. We can find precedence for this notion in the commonplace description of a great artwork as being 'timeless'. Since eternity is conceivably a dimension outside of time, a timeless quality might refer to the capacity to have a 'moment' of presence that extends into the eternal. The moment when creativity comes to visit is something which could be described as occurring within the eternal present moment. Time is directly connected to the unfolding process of music, but the creative moment itself stands outside of time. Thus, we can alter our previous definition: music is a quality that unfolds in time and emerges as a timelessly creative reconciliation between sound and silence.

THE SCIENCE OF SOUND

Sound is essentially a wave of vibrational pressure travelling through a medium in space and occurring in time. This important connection between sound and time corresponds to a fundamental characteristic of sound known as *frequency*. The frequency of a sound is determined by the number of vibrations that occur within a specified duration of time. The unit of time used to measure the frequency of sound is one second. The number of vibrations occurring within that time is referred to as either *cycles per second* (cps), or *hertz* (Hz), taken from the name of Heinrich Hertz, who demonstrated the existence of electromagnetic waves. Thus, the frequency of sound is measured in hertz and connects sound with time.

The connection between sound and space is based on the dimensions of sound waves, including length, depth, and shape. The length of a sound wave, referred to as *wavelength*, is inversely proportionate to its frequency. To put it quite simply: The longer the sound waves, the fewer vibrations will occur within a second's time and the lower they will sound; the shorter the sound waves, the more will occur within a second's time and the higher they will sound. The depth of a sound wave, referred to as *amplitude*, is the volume of a sound. Amplitude is connected to how much vibrational pressure a sound wave creates and is measured in *decibels* (dB). The shape of a sound wave, called a *waveform*, determines the *harmonic spectrum* which makes up the *tone*, *timbre*, and *texture* of a sound in addition to its *fundamental frequency*. The fundamental frequency is the definite and audibly apparent *pitch* of a sound. The tone, timbre, and texture of a sound give it unique features which distinguish it from other sounds, even those that have the same pitch.

In connection with pitch, frequency has a cyclically emergent pattern relative to different scales. This means that any frequency which produces a particular pitch can correspond to the same exact pitch on a higher or lower level. It also means that each level has a corresponding range of recurring pitches. Therefore, there are classes of the same set of pitches that exist on different scales, and there is also a recurring mathematical pattern to their frequencies. In order to find the frequency of the same pitch on a higher level, the original frequency must be doubled; to find the frequency of the same pitch on a lower level, the original frequency must be halved. Although in theory, each level or range of frequencies is infinitely divisible, musical practise uses a definite number of pitches for each level. The range of vibrational frequencies that are generally audible spans approximately ten different levels (20 Hz – 20,000 Hz). The levels below these ranges are *infrasound,* and the levels above are *ultrasound.* However, this range is relative to hearing capacities, which vary from person to person. Extremely low frequencies pass into a predominately tactile experience of pitch as a pulsation. The fundamental frequencies of infrasonic pulsation tend to be obscured by harmonics that extend upwards into the audible range. At extremely low frequencies, pulsation makes a recognizable transition into rhythm, the tempo of which is usually measured by *beats per minute* (bpm); for example, 60 bpm = 1 Hz. The ultrasonic range of frequencies can also be experienced to varying degrees through bone conduction directly into the inner ear, or through ultrasound demodulation whether by brain resonance or possibly even by the nervous system through the skin.

The term *frequency* can refer either to the number of waves measured in a specified duration of time or to the phenomena of the waves themselves. For example, sound is itself a vibrational frequency, but 440 Hz is a specific frequency of sound. Another important type of wave phenomenon is *electromagnetic frequency* (EMF). Waves of electromagnetic radiation travel through space and occur in time, and as with sound waves, the connection to time gives them measurable frequencies. The same units of measurement can be used for both sound and electromagnetic waves. Both vibrations and electromagnetic radiations can be understood as waves, but they operate with different types of energy. Therefore, they can exist in the same space and at the same frequency rates without interfering with each other. However, electromagnetic frequencies extend much higher and travel much faster than sonic frequencies, and electromagnetic waves are able to get much smaller than sound waves because they do not require a material medium (although, if light can also be understood as a particle, perhaps it provides its own medium). Because the range is so much wider, electromagnetic frequencies in the ranges common for sound waves are considered *ultra-low frequencies* or *extremely-low frequencies* (ULF or ELF). The electromagnetic frequencies we more commonly encounter are far above the transition into the ultrasonic frequency range. Going above that range, there are *long-*, *medium-*, and *short-wave* radio frequencies, *very high frequency* (VHF) radio frequencies, *ultra high frequency* (UHF) television frequencies, *micro-waves,* far and near *infrared* (IR) light, the visible light spectrum, near and far *ultraviolet* (UV) light, x-rays, gamma rays, and cosmic rays. These frequencies can become extremely large—too large to use in practical calculations or even to mentally comprehend—so they are often measured by their wavelengths instead (which only get smaller as the frequency increases). Although this conversion of frequency into wavelength (by dividing the speed of light by the frequency) makes some measurements more manageable, the wavelengths can still become so small as to convey just as little meaning as the frequency measurements. Because these wavelengths can become so small, new measurements of length had to be introduced to compensate; for example, *Ångstroms* (Å) and *nanometers* (nm). These minute measurements, along with scientific notation, allow for calculations to be carried out with inconceivably small wavelengths. However, all the measures used to compensate for the drastic proportions involved make it too easy to overlook the chief commonality between sound and electromagnetic measurements: frequency. *Therefore, I propose to standardize all frequency measurements for our purposes by converting all wavelength measurements here back into frequency (which can be done by dividing the speed of light by wavelength).* To process wavelength measurements, calculations, and data through the filter of an inversely proportionate relationship seems to complicate the matter and therefore draws attention away from important correspondences between different types of frequency. For me, using wavelength to work with frequency is something like driving a car in reverse to find one's way around town.

Light can be understood as a wave of electromagnetic radiation; thus, all the colours composing the entire visible spectrum are actually frequencies. This means that every colour we see consists of electromagnetic frequencies. The whole range of frequencies that we are able to see is exactly like a single level of pitches that we are able to hear, but on a scale that is forty times higher. The level below the visible spectrum consists of infrared light. Although we cannot see IR, we are able to experience a small portion of it as heat. The level above the visible spectrum consists of ultraviolet light. Although we cannot see ultraviolet light, we are able to experience a small portion of near UV through the phenomenon known as *flourescence* (as with the use of blacklights), and we are able to experience some far UV from its effects on the body in the form of a sunburn.

In traditional colour theory, the spectrum of visible light can be divided up in different ways. Taken together as a whole, the entire range of colour makes up white light. Divided into two parts, there are warm colours and cool colours. Divided into three parts, there are three primary colours. Divided into six parts, there are three primary and three secondary colours. Divided into seven parts, there are the seven colours of the traditional rainbow or 'ROYGBIV'. Divided into twelve parts, there are three primary, three secondary, and six tertiary colours. In theory, the range of colour is infinitely divisible, but a basic definite 'palette' of colours is used for practical purposes. When light is divided into twelve parts, such as those represented on a standard colour wheel, there are twelve distinct colours to work with (their abbreviations are placed in parenthesis):

Magenta / Crimson	(M/C)
Red	(R)
Red/Orange	(R/O)
Orange	(O)
Orange/Yellow	(O/Y)
Yellow	(Y)
Yellow/Green	(Y/G)
Green	(G)
Green/Blue	(G/B)
Blue	(B)
Indigo	(I)
Violet	(V)

However, since the light spectrum does not really contain magenta or crimson, their actual place in the spectrum corresponds to the colours *infrared* (IR) and *ultraviolet* (UV). Both are mostly invisible, and both occupy the position corresponding to magenta on the colour wheel. If the same position on the colour wheel can be seen as both the beginning and the end of the circle, then the beginning of the light spectrum can also be understood as the end of the light spectrum. The only difference is a matter of scale. Since the entire spectrum is a range of colours on a single level, then UV must be the same colour as IR on a higher scale. The same is also true with sound. If we were take a colour as the equivalent of a pitch, the very same pitch is able to recur on a higher or lower scale. As all the colours of the light spectrum are actually frequencies, we can calculate them approximately by converting them from their approximate wavelengths:

Colour	Wavelength	Frequency
Infrared	7653 Å	391,731,945,642,231.81 Hz
Red	7228 Å	414,765,437,188,710.57 Hz
Red/Orange	6818 Å	439,707,330,595,482.55 Hz
Orange	6438 Å	465,660,854,302,578.44 Hz
Orange/Yellow	6058 Å	494,870,349,950,478.71 Hz
Yellow	5736 Å	522,650,728,730,822.87 Hz
Yellow/Green	5415 Å	553,633,348,107,109.88 Hz
Green	5110 Å	586,678,000,000,000.00 Hz
Green/Blue	4823 Å	621,589,172,714,078.37 Hz
Blue	4552 Å	658,595,030,755,711.78 Hz
Indigo	4298 Å	697,516,188,925,081.43 Hz
Violet	4054 Å	739,497,923,038,973.85 Hz
Ultraviolet	3827 Å	783,361,531,225,503.00 Hz

Due to the extreme measurements involved, and because of the infinite divisibility of the colour spectrum, these calculations are merely approximate. Therefore, it must be taken into consideration that any calculations using these figures will only be roughly precise.

The first and easiest observation we can make is that the frequency for UV is roughly double that of IR. Comparing this to the frequencies of sound, it is obvious that this is verification for taking IR and UV as being the same colour on a different level as well as being equivalent to the magenta position on a colour wheel. The apparent similarities arising in the calculations between the wave properties of both sound and light are due to the fact they are both forms of frequency. Therefore, these calculations work the same and can be equally applied to both types of waves. From this correspondence, we are able to understand more about one by extrapolating from the other. By analogy, this is like using a map small enough to hold when driving to an unknown location, rather than using a large table map or even a globe. Both are accurate according to their scale; but their scales are drastically different. The differences between them makes one of them more useful than the other for the purpose of finding the way around town.

The second observation we can make has to do with the ratios of the *intervals* or distances between each of these frequencies. These ratios can be calculated by dividing the higher frequency by the lower:

IR – R:	1.0587991
R – R/O:	1.0601349
R/O – O:	1.0590245
O – O/Y:	1.0627270
O/Y – Y:	1.0561367
Y – Y/G:	1.0592798
Y/G – G:	1.0596869
G – G/B:	1.0595065
G/B – B:	1.0595342
B – I:	1.0590972
I – V:	1.0601875
V – UV:	1.0593154

The observation can be made that these ratios are approximately the same, but they are slightly inconsistent due again to the extreme measurements involved and the infinite divisibility of the spectrum. If we compare the spectrum to a colour wheel consisting of a circle divided into twelve equal parts, the twelve divisions of the colour spectrum should likewise have a single ratio. For a circle, this is done by dividing 360 degrees by twelve different 30-degree segments. To do approximately the same thing with a single level of frequencies, we must delineate twelve specific intervals at a ratio of the irrational number derived from the 12th root of 2 (1.05946309435929526456...). Since green is the only colour from the list calculated here that has a whole-number frequency, we shall use it as the fundamental frequency to calculate a single level divided into twelve equal intervals according to a single ratio:

IR	391,560,587,982,383.71 Hz
R	414,843,992,172,961.33 Hz
R/O	439,511,899,623,928.87 Hz
O	465,646,637,183,299.67 Hz
O/Y	493,335,427,108,218.74 Hz
Y	522,670,678,161,137.98 Hz
Y/G	553,750,294,015,470.58 Hz
G	586,678,000,000,000.00 Hz
G/B	621,563,689,272,522.63 Hz
B	658,523,789,578,046.32 Hz
I	697,681,651,815,566.39 Hz
V	739,167,961,710,224.40 Hz
UV	783,121,175,964,767.42 Hz

Now that we have adjusted all the ratios of the twelve intervals consistently in order to equally divide one level of frequencies, we may return to the first observation with the new figures to find that the frequency for UV is precisely double that of IR. Therefore, IR and UV are actually the same colour, as supported by the facts that they are both mostly invisible and that they fall on the same place on the colour wheel as magenta. In actuality, magenta is considered *extra-spectral* (meaning that it does not have a unique electromagnetic frequency) and is created by an optical illusion resulting from the frequencies at far ends of the visible colour spectrum blending in the eyes.

Since light and sound are both frequencies, they both operate according to similar rules. Therefore, it is possible to equally distribute twelve divisions of sound by using the same ratio used for light. It is also possible to take the frequency of a colour and lower it forty levels to correspond to the range of sonic frequencies. If we use green again, because it was initially calculated as a whole number, we can calculate this audible frequency by dividing the number by two, forty consecutive times (which is 2^{40}), resulting in 533.58 Hz. Next, we can use this number to calculate all twelve colour frequencies forty levels below by using the same ratio we used before:

IR	356.12 Hz
R	377.30 Hz
R/O	399.73 Hz
O	423.50 Hz
O/Y	448.69 Hz
Y	475.37 Hz
Y/G	503.62 Hz
G	533.58 Hz
G/B	565.31 Hz
B	598.92 Hz
I	634.54 Hz
V	672.27 Hz
UV	712.24 Hz

In practise, the same thing is done with the frequencies for musical pitches, except the standard the tuning is set at the musical note called 'A' which has been arbitrarily assigned the frequency of 440.00 Hz. According to the correspondence between sound and light, this frequency falls between the colours O/Y and Y. Therefore, when one calculates the musical frequencies by using the same ratio as before, two observable discrepancies arise:

440.00 Hz	A
466.16 Hz	
493.88 Hz	
523.25 Hz	
554.37 Hz	
587.33 Hz	
622.25 Hz	
659.26 Hz	
698.46 Hz	
739.99 Hz	
783.99 Hz	
830.61 Hz	
880.00 Hz	

The first observation is that the frequency level of sound begins on a different colour than it should according to the frequency level of light. The second observation is that the musical frequencies always land in between the colour frequencies, indicating that the standard frequency for tuning does not line up with the colour spectrum or vice versa. Both of these discrepancies are due to the arbitrariness of selecting 440 Hz as the fundamental frequency for music. It initially appears that one might suggest altering the fundamental frequency to 448.69 Hz; however, standard, readily available tuning devices only allow for a variance of 1 Hz. A practical solution would therefore be to round the new fundamental frequency up to 449 Hz. Since each of the twelve frequencies is equally divided according to the same ratio, the first frequency in the level of musical frequencies could be regarded as the pitch corresponding to IR / UV / magenta / crimson. Therefore, the new set of musical frequencies and their corresponding colours, according to this practical solution, are:

IR	356.37 Hz	
R	377.56 Hz	
R/O	400.01 Hz	
O	423.80 Hz	
O/Y	449.00 Hz	A
Y	475.70 Hz	
Y/G	503.99 Hz	
G	533.95 Hz	
G/B	565.71 Hz	
B	599.34 Hz	
I	634.98 Hz	
V	672.74 Hz	
UV	712.74 Hz	

If we take 449 Hz up forty octaves and compare it to the frequency for O/Y, we can verify the relative precision resulting from this adjustment.

449.00 Hz	493,680,720,871,424.00 Hz	(musical application with equal divisions)
O/Y	493,335,427,108,218.74 Hz	(colour application with equal divisions)
O/Y	494,870,349,950,478.71 Hz	(approximate frequency of colour)
448.69 Hz	(approximate frequency of colour down forty octaves)	

Only a relatively small difference exists between the practical solution and an equally divided colour spectrum. The differential on the musical frequency level between the original colour frequencies and the proposed tuning adaptation is less than 1 Hz. To put this into perspective, during a performance, the average musical instrument can easily drift further out of tune than this inconsequential amount. This is, therefore, a relatively precise and very practical means for harmonizing the frequency correspondence between sound and light by altering the frequency used as the basis for tuning musical instruments.

Whether 449 Hz is ever accepted as a scientifically relevant solution, or whether it is ever considered a less arbitrary alternative to the commonly used 440 Hz, the fact remains that there is a fundamental connection between colour and sound. This correspondence is one of the principal foundations for this new theory of music.

The Philosophy of Perspectives

A perspective is a particular point of view that determines how things are seen. Our own perspective determines how we see things and therefore provides a means for interpreting our experience. Therefore, our experience provides us with what we know, but our perspective shapes how we understand it. Knowledge alone does not automatically lead to understanding. Understanding often calls for a certain effort to be made in order to make the move from theory into practise. Understanding something involves making connections among particular things that we already know. One example of this is the knowledge of a language, which includes learning a specific vocabulary, grammar, set of symbols, etc. However, understanding a language means being able to connect all these elements together in such a way that communication becomes possible. Another example is someone trying to arrive at a specific destination. One can be given a particular set of directions on how to get there (which would correspond to having knowledge), but having those directions does not necessarily mean that one really understands where that location is. If one understands where something is, one might be able to find different routes to get there or even get there coming from different starting points. The different routes may even appear unrelated to one another, but they correspond in that they end up at the same location. The connection between them comes with understanding. Therefore, understanding can be regarded as the capacity to see the connections between things.

Seeing something from multiple perspectives can provide a deeper understanding of it. This can be thought of as being similar to depth perception in the same way that having two eyes slightly apart from each other gives us the capacity to perceive the three dimensions of space. A further example of this idea is that people are only able to understand others when they can see their own perspective in the context of the other person's perspective. No amount of knowing someone's perspective will make another person absolutely understand it unless he or she shares the exact same experiences and understands them in a similar way. As with the example of depth perception, understanding something from one's own point of view and from someone else's at the same time brings a whole new dimension to a relationship. Understanding is being able to really enter into another person's experience and is therefore the capacity to relate and connect with other people.

Understanding depends upon perspectives. Being able to look from different angles allows one to see the same things in new and different ways.

Some things which appear disconnected or unrelated from one angle may prove to be otherwise from another angle. Therefore, multiple perspectives are necessary for drawing lines of understanding between our points of knowledge. Since making these connections is vital to understanding something, the intentional use of multiple perspectives can be made into a valuable tool for understanding.

The obvious intent of this section is to validate this work and reveal the potential value in approaching music theory from a new perspective. From considering these ideas, one could easily conclude that looking at music theory from different perspectives might result in a greater understanding of music. At the very least, it might inspire a re-examination and re-evaluation of various elements within the existing music theory. However, the value of the idea that perspectives can be used as a tool for understanding goes beyond mere substantiation of a new approach to music. It also serves as an introduction to the idea that our perspectives are built from unique structures bearing universal patterns. The structures which comprise our perspectives are in a certain sense unknowable in themselves, but they are recognizable because they contain certain patterns which appeal directly to our understanding—that is, to our ability to see connections. This means that there are particular types of universal connections which can be both recognized and applied. This, taken together with the idea that a greater number of perspectives results in a deeper understanding, means that the more of these universal patterns we can use to make connections, the more we can understand. A perspective limited to only one pattern being applied to everything will result in a very poor and shallow understanding. Looking at things from multiple perspectives—each one using a different set of patterns—will result in a richer and deeper understanding.

These universal structures, which shape our perspectives and enrich our understanding, are related to the inherent meanings of numbers. Just as water is able to take on three distinct forms based upon the temperature of its environment, numbers are able to take on three different modes of significance based upon their context. The ordinal significance of a number conveys the order of something, such as in a sequence or hierarchy. The quantitative significance of a number conveys the quantity of something, such as is used for counting or in mathematics. The qualitative significance of a number conveys the quality of something, such as a gradation or type. Numbers are most commonly used for communicating what order something goes in or how much of something there is. However, there are also certain underlying characteristics that numbers imply which tend to go unnoticed unless special attention is given to them; and these can be spoken of as *qualities*.

Qualities are used to describe things, so it is difficult to think about a quality without also having something to attribute it to. One could say that qualities by themselves are unknowable, but that we are able to recognize and describe them nevertheless. Qualities by themselves are indefinite, unknowable, or one could even say 'spiritual', and yet they are the principal means by which we recognize things. On the other hand, orders and quantities are considered definite, knowable, or even 'scientific'. Numbers themselves are knowable, but they are recognized and understood because of their qualitative significance. To find the quality of a particular number, we have to find what it is that makes a number what it is. In other words, we need to look into the essential characteristics which are unique to each number. For example, we can pursue this by asking: What is the 'one-ness' of one? What is the 'two-ness' of two? What is the 'three-ness' of three? And so on. These questions can only be explored and answered in terms of qualities which can be divided into a corresponding number of elements. Here is an example of what can be arrived at by exploring the qualitative significance of numbers:

'One-ness' can be understood as unity, wholeness, universality, uniqueness, etc. Each of these qualities cannot be further divided; each is a single element which could be referred to as a *monad*. The element of a monad can apply to anything that has one of these qualities.

'Two-ness' can be understood as polarity, complementarity, diversity, differentiation, duality, etc. Each of these qualities can be divided into two necessary elements which could be referred to as a *dyad*. The elements of a dyad can apply to anything that has one of these qualities.

'Three-ness' can be understood as relationship, relatedness, reconciliation, unity-in-diversity, etc. Each of these qualities can be divided into three necessary elements which could be referred to as a *triad*. The elements of a triad can apply to anything having one of these qualities.

Any thing which is whole unto itself can be divided into different sets of elements that constitute these specific qualities. This makes it possible to apply universal connections between different aspects of a thing. A practical example of this is a beam of white light going through a prism.

When this happens, all the colours that make up the white light are separated into a spectrum. The colour spectrum taken as a whole (a monad) is characterized by the unity among each of the colours which together compose white light. If the colour spectrum were divided into two parts (a dyad), it would reveal two complementary sets of colours referred to as warm and cool. If the colour spectrum were divided into three parts (a triad), it would reveal primary colours. If the colour spectrum were divided into six parts (a hexad), it would reveal primary and secondary colours. If the colour spectrum were divided into seven parts (a heptad), it would reveal the traditional progression of distinct colours which were eventually labelled by Isaac Newton and whose selection we mistakenly refer to as 'ROYGBIV' (a misnomer, since what Newton called 'blue' is more accurately what we would call 'cyan', and his 'indigo' is our 'blue'). If the colour spectrum were divided into twelve parts (a dodecad), it would reveal all the colours of a colour wheel. In theory, the colour spectrum is infinitely divisible, but the colour wheel forms a complete picture of the archetypical foundations from which an artist can work on a practical level. All the colours in between can be attained by mixing these twelve colours in specific proportions. This fact is very interesting in relation to the pursuit of numerical qualities because it is probably impossible for us to attribute specific qualities to numbers higher than twelve, even though every number should theoretically have its own. Another point of interest is that just as our Hindu-Arabic numerals for ten, eleven, and twelve require combining two numerals from zero to nine, the qualities of those higher numbers can only be approached by combining qualities derived from the lower numbers. All this is interesting because it reveals to us the limits of our own understanding.

As another example, white light itself could be considered a monad since all the colours of the spectrum are united to form the beam as a whole. The spectrum on the other side of the prism contains all the colours as separate and distinct parts that make up the white light. Therefore, the beam of white light on one side and the spectrum of different colours on the other can be understood as a dyad. These two elements are related by the prism in the middle which is refracting the light. The beam of white light, the colour spectrum, and the prism form a relationship which can be understood as a triad.

The first example shows how looking at the colour spectrum from different perspectives—such as wholeness, complementarity, relatedness, etc.—was able to enrich our understanding of colour. The second example shows how we can enrich our understanding of light by applying the same set of perspectives to the elements that set up the first example. Since these different perspectives allow us to universally apply different sets of connections to any whole thing, they can become effective tools for understanding.

The formal study of the perspectives derived from the qualities of numbers was originally undertaken by the philosopher, linguist, mathematician, scientist, and historian; John G. Bennett. The ideas for what he called 'systematics' were gleaned from the esoteric teachings of Christianity along with his own research and personal experience. One of the consistently recurring themes throughout his findings was the universal significance of the numbers *three*, *seven*, and *twelve*. The following is an attempt to show the types of significances he was likely to have encountered behind these numbers.

Three conveys a universal principle that *every independent thing is the result of the combination of three cosmic forces: +, −, and =* (these symbols are universal abstractions that can be pronounced respectively as 'plus', 'minus', and 'equals'). This principle can be found on many different scales and in many different applications such as science, physics, mathematics, geometry, philosophy, linguistics, art, religion, etc. Here are some examples of this principle:

	+	−	=
Atom:	Proton	Electron	Neutron
Circuit:	Positive	Negative	Conductive Medium
Magnet:	North	South	Magnetic Material
Components:	Active	Passive	Electromechanical
Addition:	First Addend	Second Addend	Sum
Subtraction:	Minuend	Subtrahend	Difference
Multiplication:	Multiplicand	Multiplier	Product
Division:	Dividend	Divisor	Quotient
Triangle:	A	B	C
Space:	Length	Width	Depth
Coordinates:	Latitude	Longitude	Altitude
Dialectic:	Thesis	Antithesis	Synthesis
Sentence:	Subject	Object	Predicate
Family:	Father	Mother	Child
Additive Light:	Red	Blue	Green
Additive Shade:	White	Black	Grey
Subtractive Light:	Red	Blue	Yellow
Subtractive Shade:	Black	White	Grey
Lighting:	Key	Back	Fill
Primary Hue:	Red	Blue	Yellow
Musical Chord:	Root	Fifth	Third
Trinity (Christianity):	Father	Son	Holy Spirit
'Mothers' (Kabbalah):	Shin	Mem	Alef
Trimurti (Hinduism):	Brahma (Creator)	Shiva (Destroyer)	Vishnu (Preserver)
Tridevi (Hinduism):	Saraswati	Parvati/Mahakali	Lakshmi
Triguna (Sankhya):	Rajas	Tamas	Sattvas
Trikaya (Buddhism):	Dharmakaya	Sambhogayaka	Nirmanakaya
Triratna (Buddhism):	Buddha	Dharma	Sangha
Triple Bodhi (Buddhism):	Budhu	Pasebudhu	Mahaarahath
Tao (Taoism):	Yang	Yin	Tao
Pure Ones (Taoism):	Origin	Divinity	Way
(Egyptian):	Osiris	Isis/Set	Horus
(Theban/Egypitan):	Amun	Mut	Khonsu
(Memphite/Egyptian):	Ptah	Sekhmet	Nefertem

One definitely gets the intuitive sense that there is bound to be some universal principle underlying so many examples, whether or not it is something that can be objectively proven.

Seven conveys a universal principle that *every process is completed in seven distinct steps or stages according to a pattern that always contains points at which the rate of progression deviates. The irregularities in the pattern introduce hazard or uncertainty into a process, naturally causing it to go off course. The deviations from the original direction of a process can only be overcome or corrected through intelligent and intentional re-directions that come from outside the process. The final step of a process begins a new process characterized by the same recurring pattern on a higher or lower level.* Various forms of this principle can be found in religion, art, philosophy, history, and science.

For example, the idea that every process is completed in seven distinct steps reflects the original process of Creation according to the Bible, whether it is taken as an historical event, an allegorical teaching, or a mythological story. The process of Creation was described as unfolding in seven steps which were represented by the seven days of the week. Once the original process initiated by God was complete, the process began again on different levels according to the same pattern. One can easily imagine how the same process used in Creation would continue to be an underlying pattern in everything that exists, therefore making it a universal principle. This idea of seven steps or stages in a process is commonly intuited as self-evident, and its application tends to carry with it some sort of weight even without plausible explanation. For instance, Isaac Newton described the colour spectrum as having seven distinct steps. Like the colour spectrum, the most common musical scales spanning all cultures throughout all of history consist of or imply varying patterns of seven distinct steps.

The idea that there are naturally arising points of deviation or hazard in any process has been timelessly expressed by the following saying: There are no straight lines or perfect circles in nature. We encounter this principle in a host of natural phenomena including the geometric spirals found in nature, the irrational numbers of mathematics, the entropy of thermodynamics, the irrationality of subatomic particles in physics, the uncertainty principle of quantum mechanics, and many other areas that consistently elude our understanding because they are exceptions to the general rules that we have discovered. The idea of deviations in a process also relates to theological, religious, and even historical contexts. For example, the notion of the fall of humanity as relayed in the story of Eden, the tale of the fall of angels from heaven, and the prolific stories about the deviations of humanity and the Israelites throughout the Bible all stem from the same universal principle. Many deviations have also occurred within all the religions throughout history. One obvious example is the deviation of Christianity into the Crusades and the Inquisition. Only intelligent and intentional re-directions from higher, outside forces and the intervention of God can lead Creation back to its original direction.

Finally, the idea that the completion of a process begins a new process on a different level has been timelessly expressed in the ancient formulation attributed to Hermes Trismegistus: As above, so below. This is basically the notion of analogy between things on different scales relative to one another. In other words, there are similarities between higher and lower levels or between the whole and its parts. However, since there are points of deviation in every process, analogies tend to break down when stretched too far. The idea that a similar pattern recurs on different levels can be found in the relative correspondences in science between solar systems and atoms, in religion between God and humanity, or even between the colours of light and musical notes of sound as described in the previous section on frequency.

In addition to all these examples, heptads can also be found in most of the religious teachings and cultural traditions throughout the world. Here is a very brief and superficial list of heptads from various contexts:

Judaism: Creation unfolded in seven days, resulting in the seven days of the week.

Kabbalah: There are seven Hebrew letters called 'doubles' because they each have two sounds.

Christianity: There are many sevens throughout the Bible, but nowhere as obvious as in the imagery of Revelation, which includes the seven spirits of God, seven stars, seven golden lampstands, seven lamps of fire, etc.

Islam: The Quran makes references to seven heavens (which is a concept common to Christianity, Judaism, and Hinduism).

Sufism: There are seven 'lataif' (psychospiritual organs connected to subtle bodies) and seven levels of being or stages of development.

Hinduism: There is a deity named 'Agni' that is represented as having three legs, seven arms, seven tongues, and emits seven rays of light that represent the emanations of the sun.

Buddhism: There are seven sets of qualities conducive to enlightenment, among which are seven factors of enlightenment.

Yoga / Tantra: There are seven 'chakras' (energy centres connected to subtle bodies).

Taoism: There is a group of seven spirits called 'Seven Stars'.

Zoroastrianism: The highest deity named 'Ahura Mazda' along with the 'Amesha Spenta' (which are its six emanations) form a divine heptad.

Chaldean: There is a deity named 'Heptaktis' that has seven rays of light.

Twelve has the universal significance of perfection because it represents a complete range or spectrum of archetypes. It therefore conveys the universal principle of *archetypicality*. An example of this principle was mentioned earlier in the description of how the infinite divisions of the colour spectrum have been simplified into twelve archetypical divisions on the artist's colour wheel. It was also mentioned that all the theoretical colours in between can be attained by mixing these colour archetypes. Along these same lines, there are also typically twelve divisions of musical notes, even though an infinite number of divisions are theoretically possible. From this, one can conclude that the only practical way that we can grasp infinite complexity or variety is by simplifying it into archetypical divisions that fall within the limits of our own understanding. This is only possible by means of the underlying principle of archetypicality represented by the dodecad. This principle can easily be found in the division of the year into twelve months, the twelve constellations of the zodiac, the twelve astrological signs commonly connected to twelve basic personality types, and the division of time into twelve hours before noon and twelve hours after noon. Here is a very brief and superficial list of dodecads in various religious traditions throughout the world:

Judaism: There are twelve tribes of Israel.

Kabbalah: There are twelve Hebrew letters called 'elementals'.

Christianity: There are twelve apostles of Christ.

Islam: There is the hadith of twelve successors of Muhammad (Muslim rulers or 'imams').

Hinduism: There are twelve principle deities and twelve solar deities called 'Adityas'.

Buddhism: There are twelve causal links in the chain of dependent origination.

Greek Mythology: There are twelve 'gods' of Olympus.

The universal principles described by the esoteric teachings of Christianity and the overwhelming examples of the significance behind these numbers inspired Bennett to go even further and explore the possible qualities of other numbers. His explorations revealed that every number has an essential quality which provides a corresponding structural perspective that can be used for seeing universal connections. They are difficult to write about individually without giving specific examples described in terms of these qualities. Instead of going into detail, here is a summary of the qualities attributed to each of the numbers:

1 (Monad): unity, universality, wholeness, uniqueness

2 (Dyad): polarity, complementarity, diversity, differentiation, duality

3 (Triad): relationship, relatedness, reconciliation, unity-in-diversity

4 (Tetrad): activity, relativity, order, materiality

5 (Pentad): potentiality, possibilities, significance, meaning

6 (Hexad): actualization, coalescence, synchronicity, recurrence

7 (Heptad): progression, process, transformation, creation

8 (Octad): completedness, fulfillment, ideality, relative scale

9 (Ennead): harmonization

10 (Decad): integrative complementarity, polar potentiality

11 (Undecad): synergism, complementary actualizations around a single aim

12 (Dodecad): perfection, archetypicality, ordered spectrum

These numerical qualities form the different perspectives at the foundation of this new approach to music theory. Since this book will merely serve as an introduction, only the most important numbers will be explored here. It might be interesting to note that the numbers which are fundamental to understanding music are also twelve, seven, and three. However, the overall approach to this introduction will be characterized by the number one, which means that the primary perspective will be a unitive, universal, and holistic look at the basic elements of music. Anything which unnecessarily takes things apart, points out distinctions, or makes things more complicated will be intentionally and purposefully omitted. Where this is not possible, the aim is to approach it according to the number three by showing the relationships between different elements and also how they work together as a whole.

A New Theory of Music

12

In music, only twelve notes exist. The twelve notes that exist make up the *chromatic scale*.

Many musically trained people, including musicians, composers, teachers, theorists, musicologists, and ethnomusicologists, may dispute the statement that only twelve notes exist. I simply request a momentary suspension of any preconceptions as I attempt to elucidate what is meant by this principle. For all practical purposes, a majority of music throughout the world and throughout history either makes use of or theoretically implies the existence of twelve sonically distinct classes of pitch. This can be easily concluded by looking beyond the relatively exceptional exotic scales and the relatively minor variations of musical tunings. The flexibility necessary for such a universal assertion is the reason why this should be taken as a principle rather than a rule.

Traditionally, there are seventeen different names for these notes (and more are theoretically possible), depending on how they are used. This is due to the conventional methods that have developed for recording music in a written form by means of a specialized notation. *I propose to discard all the superfluous names that refer to sonically identical notes simply by referring to the twelve distinct notes with only twelve different names.* This is merely a logical simplification which seems too obvious to have been overlooked by so many people and for such a long period time.

This is a list of the commonly used names for all twelve notes that exist. The list uses my proposed simplification in ascending and alphabetical order. (In the third column, there is a guide to pronouncing the names of the notes which differ from the English alphabet.):

1 A

2 A# 'A-sharp'

3 B

4 C

5 C# 'C-sharp'

6 D

7 D# 'D-sharp'

8 E

9 F

10 F# 'F-sharp'

11 G

12 G# 'G-sharp'

In an earlier section, we observed a frequency correspondence between the colours of the light spectrum and the musical notes of the chromatic scale. One practical way to use this correspondence is to rename and reorder the musical notes. This is a reordered list of the simplified note names along with their colours and abbreviated names:

1	F	Magenta	M
2	F#	Red	R
3	G	Red/Orange	R/O
4	G#	Orange	O
5	A	Orange/Yellow	O/Y
6	A#	Yellow	Y
7	B	Yellow/Green	Y/G
8	C	Green	G
9	C#	Green/Blue	G/B
10	D	Blue	B
11	D#	Indigo	I
12	E	Violet	V

For the purpose of introducing a new theory, only the simplified conventional names will be used to assist those who are already familiar with the traditional theory of music. For those who are not familiar with the standard note names, the best way to become acquainted with them is to imagine additional letters coming between the first seven letters of the alphabet (A, B, C, D, E, F, and G). Each imaginary letter uses the same letter as the note preceding it, but with an added '#' (pronounced 'sharp'). There are only two exceptions that do not have imaginary letters; between the letters B and C and between the letters E and F. Thus, the musical alphabet has five extra 'letters' (A#, C#, D#, F#, and G#).

All the notes are listed here with spaces inserted to emphasize the two missing exceptions within the musical alphabet:

A

A#

B

C

C#

D

D#

E

F

F#

G

G#

Since the notes of the chromatic scale are actually equally proportioned, it is more accurate to think of them without these spaces, once one has memorized them all. At this point, it is worth noting that even with the aforementioned simplifications, this way of naming the notes is completely arbitrary and fails to accurately convey anything about their equidistant relationships to one another. This point is worth taking into consideration with regards to the proposition of using the colour spectrum as a new way of naming notes instead.

After reaching G# in the list, the next note up will be another A that will begin the exact same sequence on the next higher level. This linear sequence appears only once on each and every level because only twelve notes exist and are able to maintain their unique identities on multiple levels. This means that musical instruments which are able to produce a great number of notes are really only able to produce twelve distinct notes, but they are able to do so on higher or lower levels. Therefore, if an instrument can produce thirty-six notes, it is really only capable of producing twelve distinct notes on three different levels.

To summarize: There is a linear sequence of twelve equally divided musical notes that repeat cyclically on multiple levels. Since the notes are cyclical, all levels can be included by representing the notes as twelve equally spaced points around a circle.

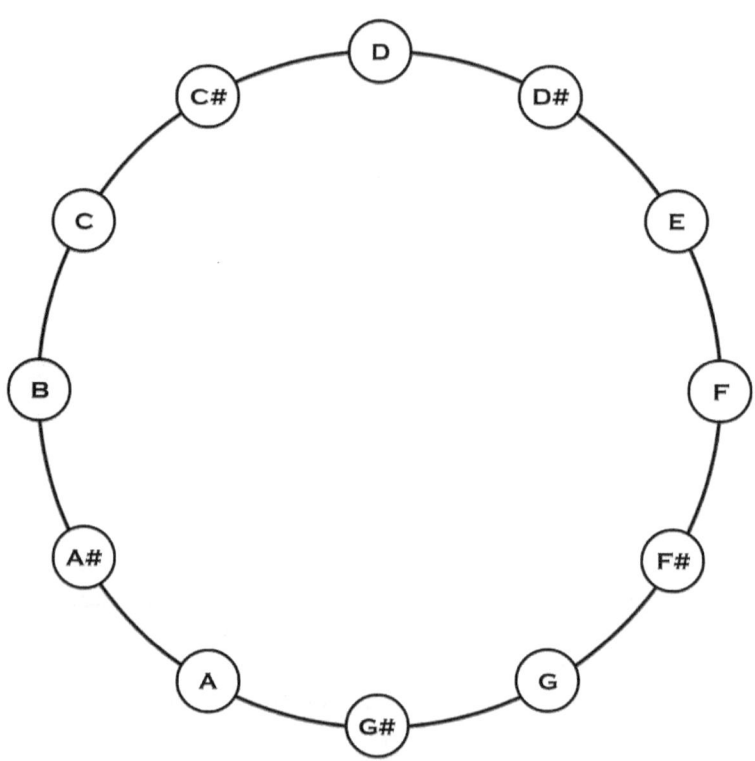

7

In a musical key, only seven notes exist. The seven notes of a key compose the primary musical scale.

Many musically trained people may dispute the statement that only seven notes exist in a scale. I simply request a momentary suspension of any preconceptions as I give an explanation similar to the one in the last chapter. For all practical purposes, a majority of music throughout the world and throughout history either makes use of or theoretically implies the existence of seven notes in a scale. This can be easily concluded by looking beyond the relatively exceptional exotic scales and musical tunings. Again, this assertion is supposed to be a universally applicable principle rather than a hard-and-fast rule.

The first note of this scale is the key-note, which can be referred to as the '1'. The notes in the scale are governed by the key-note according to a specific pattern of *intervals*, or the distances between each of the notes. The seven scale-notes always follow a fixed pattern relative to the key-note. Since the scale pattern is the same for any key based upon which note begins the scale, the individual names of the notes are interchangeable with their relative positions in the scale. The relationships of the notes to one another within the scale-pattern give them their musical significance and reveal their particular musical identities.

In order for us to keep the essential musical identities of the notes in perspective, I propose to drop each of their individual names and adopt a very simple numerical naming system that is based upon their order in the scale and independent of any particular key. The notes can be referred to by their ordinal number once a transition has been made from the twelve-note chromatic scale to the seven-note scale of a musical key. This proposal not only eliminates the necessity for learning twelve different sets of seven-note scales, but also simplifies the traditional means for universally naming the notes of the scale pattern. The antiquated naming system for doing this is called 'Solfege' and uses specific sounds to symbolize the notes in the scale. Although these sounds were adapted from a Gregorian chant and are replete with inner meaning, it is much easier to recognize order by actually using ordinal numbers.

To summarize: **The seven notes of any key can be referred to by the number of their relative position in the scale pattern.** (The Solfege names are included in the right column):

'1'	Do (originally 'Ut')
'2'	Re
'3'	Mi
'4'	Fa
'5'	Sol
'6'	La
'7'	Si (replaced by 'Ti' in contemporary use)
'1' / 8	Do

After reaching 7, the pattern repeats so that the next note is called '1' even though it is also the eighth note that completes the scale. Because the last note is the eighth note on the original level and the first note on a higher level, it is called the 'octave'. The term *octave* can refer to either the same note on a different level or an entire level of notes.

The scale pattern is best learned by breaking it into two sections according to its intervals. To do this, it is necessary to make an important observation regarding the distances between the notes going up the scale:

1-2	Two-note interval (one note is skipped)
2-3	Two-note interval (one note is skipped)
3-4	One-note interval
4-5	Two-note interval (one note is skipped)
5-6	Two-note interval (one note is skipped)
6-7	Two-note interval (one note is skipped)
7-1	One-note interval

Notice the two points of discontinuity encountered in ascending the musical scale. The rate of progression going up the scale slows down between 3 and 4 and again between 7 and 1. The irregularities in the intervals of the ascending scale are vital in helping us break the scale down into these two sections:

| Section One: | 1 – 2 – 3 |
| Section Two: | 4 – 5 – 6 – 7 |

The dashes indicate a note which must be skipped to arrive at the next note in the scale. The transitions between sections are the only places where there are no skipped notes. By including the numbers and dashes, we can observe that all twelve notes are accounted for within the pattern governing the seven notes in any key.

Here we can see the pattern for two complete octaves when both sections are combined and repeated (a dash indicates a skipped note):

1 – 2 – 3 4 – 5 – 6 – 7 1 – 2 – 3 4 – 5 – 6 – 7 1

The traditional names of the notes, their written form, and their layout on a piano were all devised to access precisely this scale pattern. However, in making the pattern more easily accessible for a particular key such as the key of C, severe handicaps were placed on our ability to access all of the other keys. Musicians typically overcome this difficulty by learning twelve different versions of the same scale. Superfluous note names and convoluted notations are the unfortunate side effects of this approach. All these problems can be solved by simply approaching music in a new way. In order to further understand why making one key easily accessible limits access to the other keys, we can make some simple observations using the musical alphabet:

1	C
2	D
3	E
4	F
5	G
6	A
7	B
1	C

Because certain notes are skipped according to the scale pattern, there are five notes found outside of the key:

1

\- C#/Db

2

\- D#/Eb

3

4

\- F#/Gb

5

\- G#/Ab

6

\- A#/Bb

7

1

These five notes are sometimes called 'accidentals' and are individually referred to as 'sharps' if accessed from the notes below or 'flats' if accessed from the notes above. The difficulty comes from altering the notes in the key of C to access the other keys. Each key uses a different set of accidentals, a different quantity of them, and different means for accessing them. This results in the necessity to refer to notes by names specific to a key, to transcribe notes by means of specific placements of specific numbers of specific symbols, and to use special maneuvering techniques to navigate specific scale patterns on a musical instrument. Such extreme specificity makes the standard approach to music debilitating in a practical context. In this new approach, the same seven numbers can represent any particular key, and any of the accidentals can be represented by combining the preceding number with a half, as illustrated below:

1
- 1.5
2
- 2.5
3
4
- 4.5
5
- 5.5
6
- 6.5
7

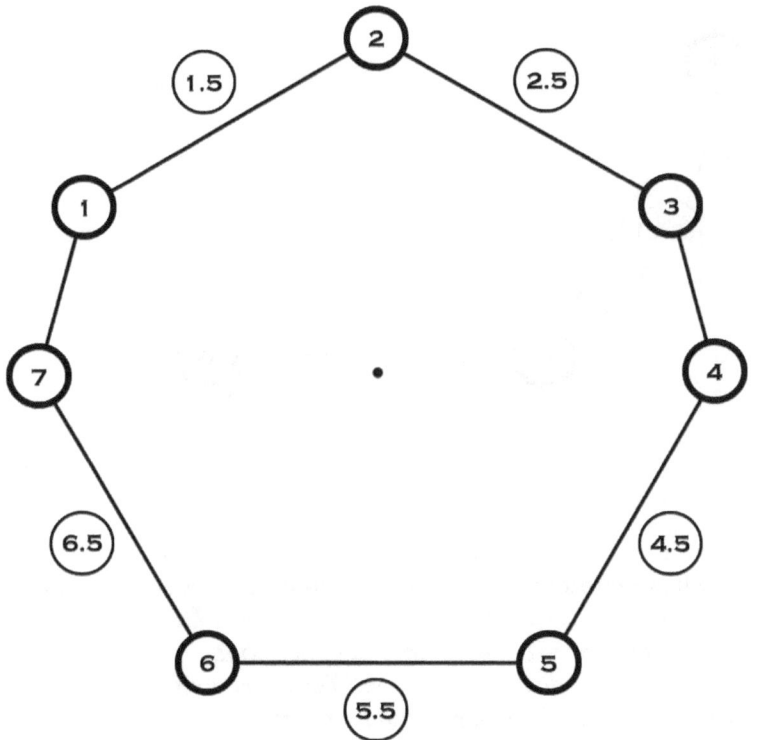

In order to understand how a key of seven notes relates to the twelve notes that exist, something like a colour wheel may be used with a geometric figure connecting the different notes according to the relationship of the intervals. If the geometric figure is placed on an independently moveable transparency with a fixed centre, it can be rotated to reveal how a single unchanging pattern of seven notes works with all twelve possible keys.

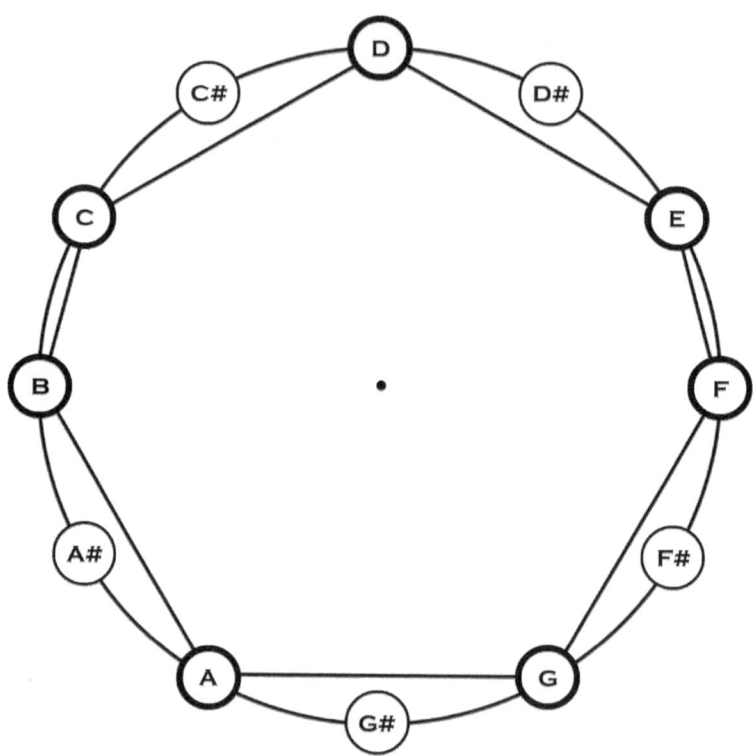

This pattern can be applied as the framework for a new musical notation when represented in a readable and linear format. *The linear format I propose consists of markings that may be placed on a grid of seven horizontal spaces between lines designed to indicate the intervals. The seven spaces are divided into two different sections based upon the irregularities of the scale pattern. The first section has three spaces that represent, from lowest to highest, the notes 1, 2, and 3. The second section (which can be shaded grey to help with the initial orientation) has four spaces that represent the remaining notes: 4, 5, 6, and 7. Dividing the two*

sections from one another are thick lines that indicate the points of discontinuity in the pattern where there is a note missing between 3 and 4 and between 7 and 1. To divide the other notes, there are thin, staff-like lines which can be marked on exactly like the spaces to indicate the notes outside of the key. The key can be represented by simply including the name (or colour) of the key in the margins. Multiple octaves can be represented by repeating the pattern vertically and specifying the number of each octave according to 'scientific musical notation'. In this way, all note markings are universally applicable to any key, thus rendering notational 'transposition' completely obsolete.

3

The most basic musical chord is a triad. In this fundamental chord, only three notes exist. Chords are the atomic elements of music, having a polarity in themselves and in their related scales. The three notes of the root chord are the primary centres of gravity within the scale. Each of the three notes plays a unique role in the whole of a chord:

'1'   +   (dominant / active / positive / affirming)

'2'   −   (subordinate / passive / negative / denying)

'3'   = or +/−   (intermediate / neutralizing / reconciling)

I propose that in the very beginning of an introduction to music, these symbols be used to represent the notes constructing a basic chord so as to indicate the roles they play, rather than using the standard names of their intervallic relationships to one another, which are better suited for more advanced applications.

The 1 of a chord is referred to as the 'root'.

The 2 of a chord is commonly referred to as the 'fifth' because its distance from the root is the same as scale-note 5 from scale-note 1 of a key.

The 3 of a chord is commonly referred to as the 'third' because its distance from the root is the same as scale-note 3 from scale-note 1 of a key.

One of the special properties of chord-note 3 is that it can be either + or −, which means that it determines the polarity of the chord as a whole. It is in connection with this polarity that + can be called 'major' and − can be called 'minor', as is done in standard music theory.

The relationship of the notes in a chord to one another is based on the intervals between them. In relation to the twelve notes that exist, chord-note 1 is simply called whatever scale-note it is named after. Chord-note 2 can almost always be found by ascending seven notes (skipping six) from chord-note 1 when working within the same octave. The +3 (pronounced 'major third') of a chord can always be found by ascending four (skipping three) from chord-note 1. The −3 (pronounced 'minor third') of a chord can always be found by ascending three (skipping two) from chord-note 1. Here is the chord construction formula:

1   +   This note names the chord based on which scale-note it uses.

2   −   This note almost always has the same relationship to chord-note 1.

3   =   This note can be either + or − and determines the polarity of the chord.

Therefore, the name of a chord always includes the note name of chord-note 1 and the polarity of chord-note 3. Chord-note 2 is assumed, often making it unnecessary to include it in the chord name.

In order to understand how a chord of three notes relates to the twelve notes that exist, something like a colour wheel may be used with a geometric figure connecting the different notes according to the relationship of the intervals. If the geometric figure is placed on an independently moveable transparency with a fixed centre, it can be rotated to reveal how the pattern of three notes works with the twelve notes that exist.

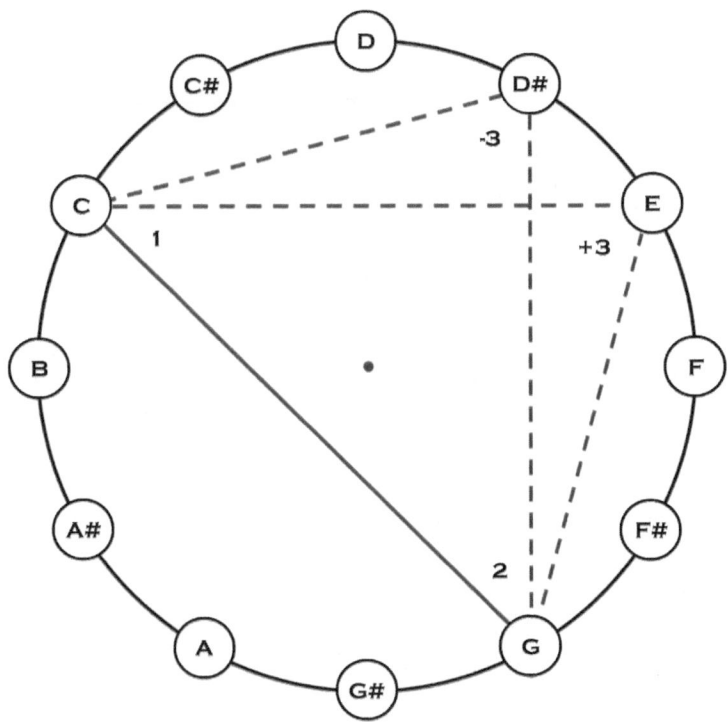

The twelve notes that exist, taken together with the variable polarity of the chord triads, yield a total of twenty-four basic chords that exist.

If we wish to bring chords into the musical context, we must take them in relation to the seven notes that exist in a musical key. Using the pattern of the scale, we can see another relationship between the notes of the basic chord triad. The intervals between them are regular in relation to the notes of the scale pattern. Chord-note 1 is the same as before, except that there are only seven scale-notes it may use. Chord-note 3 is always two scale-notes above chord-note 1 (skipping one) or two scale-notes below chord-note 2 (skipping one). Chord-note 2 is always four scale-notes above chord-note 1 or two scale-notes above chord-note 3. Chord-note 3, playing the role of = in the triad, actually mediates between the + and the − and does so at apparently equal distances between them in the scale. Just taking the seven scale-notes sequentially, chord 1 would look like this:

Scale-notes:	1	2	3	4	5	6	7
Triadic roles:	+		=		−		
Chord-notes:	1		3		2		

However, since the scale actually contains points of discontinuity, it would more accurately look like this:

Scale-notes:	1	2	3	4	5	6...
Triadic roles:	+		=		−	
Chord-notes:	1		3		2	

It does not matter what note the chord begins with, so long as it remains inside the key (triadic roles are at the top, the chord names are to the left, and the scale-notes used in the chords are in the middle from left to right):

	+	=	−
1:	1	3	5
2:	2	4	6
3:	3	5	7
4:	4	6	1
5:	5	7	2
6:	6	1	3
7:	7	2	4

From this, we can see that many of the same scale-notes are used in multiple chords and in multiple octaves, which can be better represented like this (the scale is on the left, the chord numbers are on the bottom, and the scale-notes used in the chords are in the middle):

Scale	1	2	3	4	5	6	7
4							4
3						3	
2					2		2
1				1		1	
7			7		7		7
6		6		6		6	
5	5		5		5		
4		4		4			
3	3		3				
2		2					
1	1						

However, due to the irregularities of the scale pattern itself, there is a more complicated yet more accurate way to represent the relationship between the chords and the scale-notes used to construct them (the scale pattern is on the left, the chord numbers are at the bottom, and the scale-notes used in the chords are in the middle):

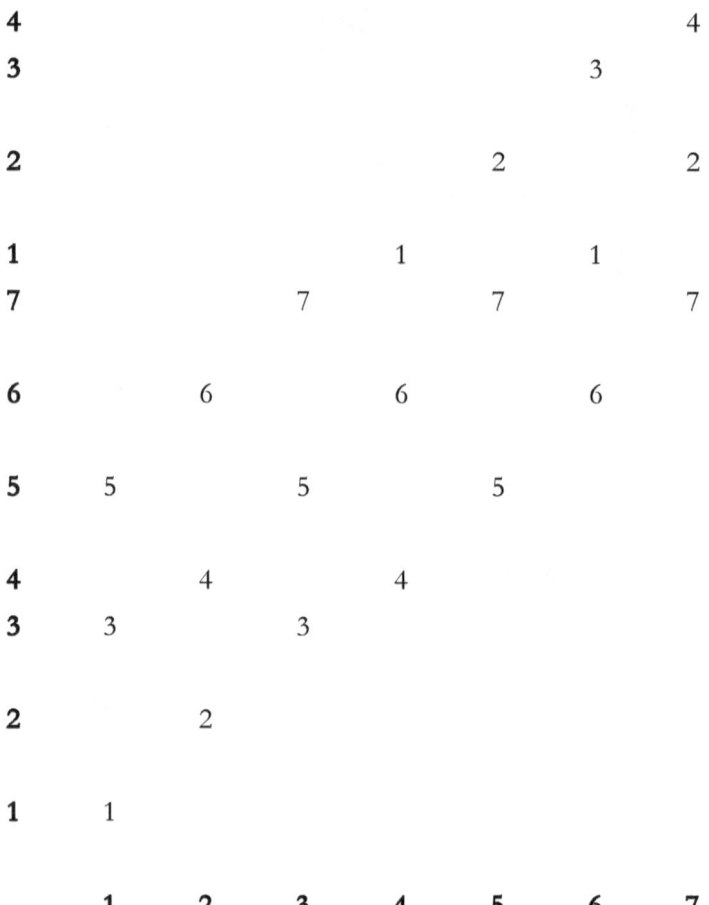

There is an underlying pattern here that may not be very obvious from this list. The best way to show how a chord relates to a key is by superimposing onto the scale pattern the chord-construction transparency that can rotate around an axis. By imagining a rotation of the chord pattern, one can observe how the distances between the chord-notes would change depending on where they land in the scale pattern:

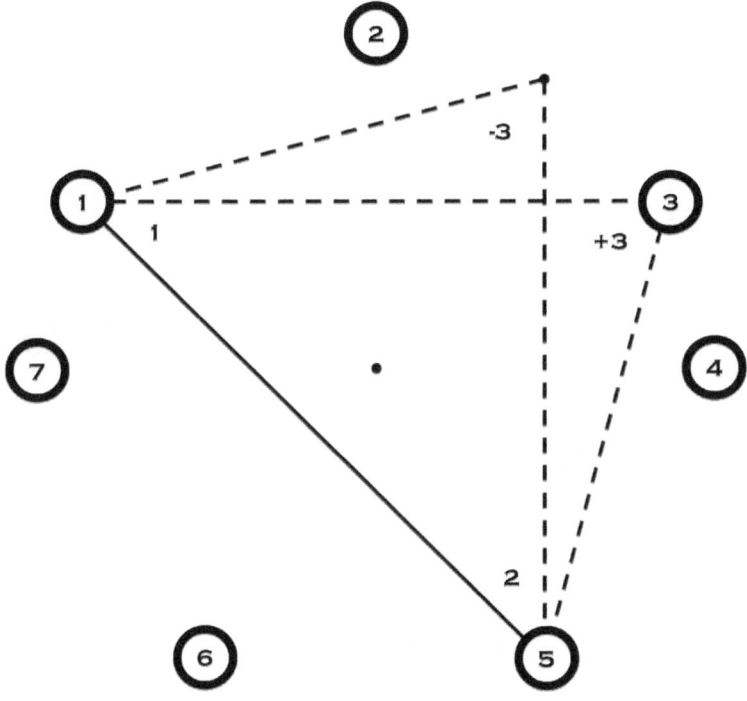

To accentuate the underlying pattern, the following chart shows the distances between the chord-notes (the distances between the notes are at the top, the chord numbers are to the left, and in the middle are both the notes used from the key and their resulting triadic roles):

	0	1up	2up	3up	4up	5up	6up	7up
	+			−	+			=
1:	1				3			5
	+				+			−
2:	2			4				6
	+			−				−
3:	3			5				7
	+			−				−
4:	4				6			1
	+				+			−
5:	5				7			2
	+				+			−
6:	6			1				3
	+			−				−
7:	7			2			4	
	+			−			−	

From this table, we can observe three different categories of chords: +, −, and =. There are three different chords in which chord-note 3 turns out to be + (chords 1, 4, and 5) and three different chords in which chord-note 3 turns out to be − (chords 6, 2, and 3). And last, there is a single chord in which chord-note 2 is not in its normal position (which is supposed to be seven chromatic notes higher than chord-note 1). Since chord-note 2 is lower than it is supposed to be, it is commonly referred to as being 'diminished'. This deviation of chord 7 falls outside the general principle of the basic chord triad and can therefore be further examined among the more advanced concepts of this music theory. But before we place chord 7 aside, we shall examine its role in a key. Since the overall polarity of the chord is determined by the polarity of chord-note 3, we can see the triadic roles of the chords themselves within a particular key:

+	−	=
1	6	7
4	2	
5	3	

This means that there are three + chords, three − chords, and one = chord. Now that we understand their roles, we can take a look at the order in which they appear:

+	−	−	+	+	−	=
1	2	3	4	5	6	7

The polarity of each chord remains the same as long as the musical context remains strictly within a single key. By sticking to the basic chord triads and excluding the exceptional chord 7, we see that only six authentic chords exist in a musical key. As long as we remain strictly within the key, the polarities of the six chords will always remain the same. *Since the polarity of each chord remains constant, I propose that it is unnecessary to specify polarity when referring to chords in a key, unless an exception arises.*

To summarize: **There are only six basic chord triads in a key. These chords are referred to by the number of the note used as chord-note 1. This number can also be used to distinguish whether a chord is + or −.** If the chords deviate from the key, the polarity should be specified in addition to the chord name. This is the list of all six basic chords that exist in a key with their understood polarities and spaced to reflect their relative position in the scale pattern of a key:

1	2	3	4	5	6
+	−	−	+	+	−

It is important to understand that each of these numbers signifies a triadic combination of notes and that all of them use the seven notes of a key as the palette as well as maintain a consistent relationship to one another.

In order to understand the polarities of chords in relation to where they are in a key, two intersecting triangles can be used to reconstruct the scale pattern representing the three + chords and the three − chords.

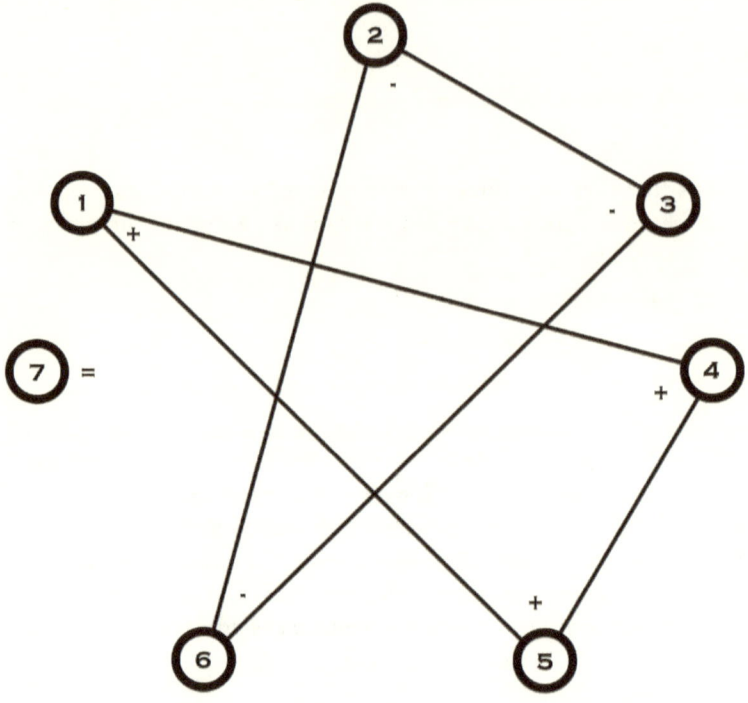

Each of the three + and three – chords can also be seen as complementary pairs. Although each chord has its own separate identity, the chords can also be thought of as related couples. All together, they form three different chord pairs.

In relation to the twelve notes that exist, the root notes of each chord in a pair are always separated by three chromatic notes. Chord-note 1 of a + chord is always three notes above (skipping two notes) chord-note 1 of its related – chord; and chord-note 1 of a – chord is always three notes below (skipping two notes) the chord-note 1 of its related + chord.

In relation to the seven notes that exist in a key, the complementary pairs are always two notes apart (skipping one note in the scale). Here are the three complimentary pairs according to their polarities:

+	−
1	6
4	2
5	3

These chords are relatively interchangeable because they each share two of the same scale-notes.

Chords 1 and 6 share scale-notes 1 and 3

Chords 4 and 2 share scale-notes 4 and 6

Chords 5 and 3 share scale-notes 5 and 7

By separating things into dyads, such as with these complementary pairs of chords, we reveal a world of unfathomable diversity and relativity. Approaching music from that type of perspective provides increased differentiation, allowing one to find many distinct parts within an integrated whole (which is a move from the universal to the particular). Since this introduction aims to present musical elements from a unified or related perspective, only the divergent aspects that prove to be practical for understanding how music works will be presented here. From the perspective of unity, a musical key maintains the existence of one scale that always contains the same seven notes. Diversity becomes apparent when each chord in the key is taken as a relative tonal centre of gravity with a distinct sound or *tonality*.

The presence of a chord colours the seven notes of a key in its own unique way. Another way of relating this to what has already been explained is that the three notes of a particular chord become the most important notes out of the seven. Chord-note 1 is the most important, followed by chord-note 3 and then chord-note 2. Since the chord-note 1 carries the most weight, it has the strongest gravitational pull towards it compared to all the other notes in the key. If we maintain the pattern of seven notes in the same order, but begin on whichever note has the most important centre of gravity, we can proceed through the same set of notes and arrive back where we started. If we do this with all six basic chords, we can distinguish between six different implied scales or *modes* within a single musical key. We can even include the anomalous chord 7 to reveal a seventh pseudo-mode. However, it is important to keep in mind that these modes are merely implied when working within the context or presence of chords. The seven modes reveal a diversity or relativity within a single key in the same way that there can be as many different stories as there are eye witnesses to a single event. To continue this analogy, once we have evidence concerning what really happened, each of the individual testimonies have less significance for us.

In traditional music theory the seven different modes are referred to by their Greek names. I propose that these be dropped entirely because they are of no practical use and do not even accurately correspond to the ancient use of their names. There is no practical reason to deeply explore the seven modes in this introduction beyond gaining a general understanding of what they are and how they work. Here is a list of the seven modes with my proposed names, what scale-notes they use, and their standardized Greek names, all arranged to show how they relate to the scale pattern:

Mode 1 (scale-notes 1-1)   Ionian

Mode 2 (scale-notes 2-2)   Dorian

Mode 3 (scale-notes 3-3)   Phrygian

Mode 4 (scale-notes 4-4)   Lydian

Mode 5 (scale-notes 5-5)   Myxolydian

Mode 6 (scale-notes 6-6)   Aeolian

Mode 7 (scale-notes 7-7)   Locrian

1	2	3	4	5	6	7	**1**
2	3	4	5	6	7	1	**2**
3	4	5	6	7	1	2	**3**
4	5	6	7	1	2	3	**4**
5	6	7	1	2	3	4	**5**
6	7	1	2	3	4	5	**6**
7	1	2	3	4	5	6	**7**

One observation that can be made is that there is no reason to memorize all seven different scale patterns for each mode, because all of them use the same set of seven notes beginning at a different place in the scale. Therefore, it is only necessary to become sufficiently familiar with mode 1 in order to have access to the others. The only practical difference is the chord context in which the same seven notes are placed. In fact, mode 1 is simply the exact same scale as the scale pattern of the key. *In standard*

*music theory the first note of each mode is taken as the 1 for its
corresponding unique scale pattern. I propose that all seven modes should
be understood as already built into the original scale pattern simply by
beginning and ending on a different note in the key. The seven modes do
not need to be studied separately except with regards to their different
advanced applications.*

Returning to the chords themselves from which each of the modes emerge,
if we take into consideration that it is chord-note 3 which determines
polarity, then chord-note 3 also becomes important in determining the
polarities of the modes. This is a list of the modes along with their
polarities:

Mode 1	(scale-notes 1-1)	+
Mode 2	(scale-notes 2-2)	−
Mode 3	(scale-notes 3-3)	−
Mode 4	(scale-notes 4-4)	+
Mode 5	(scale-notes 5-5)	+
Mode 6	(scale-notes 6-6)	−
Mode 7	(scale-notes 7-7)	=

Therefore, the modes have the same polarities as their respective chords.
Also, notice that mode 7 is = because the tonal centres of gravity are the
notes of chord 7, which does not have chord-note 2 in the normal position.
Both chord 7 and mode 7 are deviations from the norm and can therefore
be regarded as theoretical.

Like chords, each of the three + modes and three − modes can be taken
together to form complementary pairs:

+	−
1	6
4	2
5	3

If mode 1 is the same as the musical key, then there are two conceivable
names for a key. The actual name of a key is derived from the 1 (which is
+); therefore, the 6 (being the relative −) could theoretically be used as an
alternative name for that key. Mode 1 is commonly referred to as the '+
scale' and mode 6 is commonly referred to as the '− scale'. *I propose that
the fundamental characteristic of a key is that it contains the seven tones of*

the basic scale. With regards to the specific name of a key, since there is no difference between the notes in the key of 1+ and the key of 6–, I propose to simplify naming the key by always referring to the + and implying the –. Once this is done, there is no need for a so-called 'minor key'. The relative minor is always implied at the mention of the major, just as light implies the existence of darkness. Of course, this simplification also intentionally implies that the so-called 'harmonic' and 'melodic' scales are themselves exceptions rather than the rule, which is so because they introduce notes outside of the key. These exceptional scales and deviations from the norm belong to the more advanced aspects of music theory.

All these natural polarities emerge from looking at the dyadic aspects of music. In so far as it reveals diversity, this perspective can enrich our knowledge of music. However, understanding music requires experiencing the relationships between its many different parts and learning how they work together as a whole.

Rhythm

A *measure* or *bar* is the time frame in which a rhythm unfolds. A measure is made up of a number of countable pulses occurring at intervals of a relatively low frequency. Because the frequency is low, it is usually measured in the number of *beats per minute* (bpm). A *beat* is simply any count that is being used for something. In this case, the count is being used as the pulse. The number of pulses occurring within a minute determines the *tempo* (or the speed of the music). Therefore, tempo is determined by the frequency of the musical pulse.

In approaching rhythm, it is important to understand that the pulse is felt in the body and the count is followed with the mind. All of the bodily processes work in cycles; for example, heart rate, breath rate, brainwave rates, sleeping patterns, and menstrual cycles. Therefore, the pulse is natural for the body and is even a fundamental sign of life. The mind is capable of relating to time in a unique way; bringing together contact with the past through memory, direct experience of the present, and the ability to look forward to the future. The experience of the body is stuck within the present moment and moves in time. Such as it is, the body lacks the capacity to keep a picture of a whole event because it cannot maintain sufficient contact with both the beginning and the end in relation to where it is at a particular moment. Harmonizing the efforts of the body (feeling the cycles of time as they correspond to the pulse) with the efforts of the mind (holding a picture of the pattern and keeping track of its place within it) is the key to the execution of rhythm.

Returning to the time frame in which a rhythm unfolds, a bar is made up of a specified number of counts at a specified tempo. Since a tempo is really a frequency just like a musical note, the pulse can also be divided by two and remain the same tempo on a lower octave; or it may be multiplied by two in order to become the same tempo on a higher octave. The *counts*, or counting done in a bar, are usually on a higher octave than the pulse (which is traditionally referred to as 'half-time'). Counting on a higher octave in *doubles* (which is traditionally referred to as 'double-time') can operate as a general template for how a bar can be filled up with notes. Regardless of how a bar is counted, each of the beats coinciding with a count (traditionally called 'down-beats') has a + polarity and the beats in between (traditionally called 'up-beats') have a − polarity. Therefore, the pulse has the strongest beats, coinciding with the count, and double-time has weaker beats that fill up spaces between the counts. The pulse often helps divide a bar or multiple bars into + and − parts; the first section being + and the second section −. If a bar has an even number of counts, then the pulse coincides with the beginning of each measure. In effect, this neutralizes the polarity within a single bar. However, if a bar has an odd number of counts, then at least two bars are required to reconcile the shifting pulse.

Here is a chart showing an example of a bar with an even-numbered count:

4-counts 1-time

Bar-Polarity:	+			−			
Pulse-Count:	1			2			
Pulse-Polarity:	+		−		+		−
Count:	1		2		3		4
Count-Polarity:	+	−	+	−	+	−	+	−
Double-Time:	1	2	3	4	5	6	7	8

Here is a chart showing an example of two bars with an odd-numbered count (and since both bars are necessary for the pulse to coincide with a 1, they each have a polarity):

5-count 2-times (which is essentially the same as a 10-count 1-time)

Count: **1**	2	3	4	5	*1*	2	3	4	5
Pulse: **1**		2		3		4		5	
Bar: **1+**					*2−*				

As one can see from these two examples, the standard pulse is dyadic because each pulse consists of two counts. This is why a bar with an odd number of counts requires an even number of measures. However, if a bar has a number of counts divisible by three, then the optional triadic pulse (or a pulse consisting of three counts) becomes possible.

In a bar whose count is divisible by three, there is an option between using the dyadic pulse on every two counts, as in the previous examples, or the triadic pulse on every three counts. First, I shall give an example of the pulse on every two beats with a 3-count bar:

3-count 2-times (which is essentially the same as a 6-count 1-time)

Count:	1	2	3	*1*	2	3
Pulse:	1		2		3	
Bar:	1+			*2–*		

Next, I shall give an example of the pulse on the first count of two 3-count bars:

3-count 2-times (which is essentially the same as a 6-count 1-time)

Count:	1	2	3	*1*	2	3
Pulse:	1			*1*		
Bar:	1			*2*		

As you can see, the first example requires two bars for the pulse to line back up with the 1. But in the second example, there is only one pulse that changes with the one of every new bar. Furthermore, the number of times the count of a bar is divisible by three determines how many triadic pulses it has.

So let's take a look at a 6-count bar with a triadic pulse (which is essentially the same as counting 3+3):

6-count 1-time

Count:	1	2	3	4	5	6
Pulse:	1			2		
Bar:	1					

Since six can be divided twice by three, there are two triadic pulses for each bar. This means that there can also be three dyadic pulses for each bar:

6-count 1-time

Count:	1	2	3	*4*	5	6
Pulse:	1		2		3	
Bar:	1					

Six, being an even number, allows the dyadic pulse to line back up every bar. At the same time, the ability of the six to be divided by three also allows a triadic pulse to line back up with every bar. It works either way, but the difference lies in the feel of the rhythms occurring within the bar. Since the feel of the dyadic pulse is probably the more common basis for rhythm, a triadic pulse must be specified when communicating rhythms with a triadic foundation.

Timing and duration are how musical notes relate to rhythm. A single note or multiple notes can take place on any specified count and last for any specified amount of time. The counts being used for a rhythm will be referred to as beats. A full-length note begins on a beat and has the duration of a specified number of beats. There are also different lengths of beat-durations that depend on how the bar is being counted. *Count-beats* can have the duration of a 1-count (or theoretically 2 double-beats, 4 quad-beats, 8 octo-beats, 16 double-octo-beats, 32 quad-octo-beats, 64 octo-octo-beats, etc.). *Pulse-beats* have the duration of one pulse (whether dyadic or triadic) and usually lines up with the tempo. *Bar-beats* have the duration of one bar (regardless of how many counts there may be). An *extended-length note* exceeds the length of one bar and can be measured by counted-beats, pulse-beats, or bar-beats. A *partial-length note* (traditionally called 'staccato') takes into account only the beat it lands on and is cut indefinitely short. A *short-length note* (usually called 'pizzicato') functions the same as a partial-length note, but is cut even more abruptly short. With regards to full-length notes, this is a list of possible counted-beat durations:

A more complete list of possible durations can now be presented:

1-beat   (lasting for one count)

2-beat   (also one standard dyadic pulse)

3-beat   (also one triadic pulse and also traditionally called a 'dotted-note')

4-beat   (also a 2-pulse)

5-beat

6-beat   (also a 3-pulse, and traditionally another form of 'dotted-note')

7-beat

8-beat   (also a 4-pulse)

…

N-beat   (The variable indicates that any number may be used because there is no theoretical limit to the duration of a note.)

Short   (which can be notated by a 'S' beneath the count)

Partial   (which can be notated by a 'P' beneath the count)

Full:

1-quad	(.25-beat)		
1-double	(.50-beat)	2-quad	
3-quad	(.75-beat)		
1-beat		**4-quad**	**2-double**
5-quad	(1.25-beat)		
3-double	(1.50-beat)	6-quad	
7-quad	(1.75-beat)		
2-beat		**8-quad**	**4-double (1-pulse)**
9-quad	(2.25-beat)		
5-double	(2.50-beat)	10-quad	
11-quad	(2.75-beat)		
3-beat		**12-quad**	**6-double**
13-quad	(3.25-beat)		
7-double	(3.50-beat)	14-quad	
15-quad	(3.75-beat)		
4-beat		**16-quad**	**8-double (2-pulse)**
17-quad	(4.25-beat)		
9-double	(4.50-beat)	18-quad	
19-quad	(4.75-beat)		
5-beat		**20-quad**	**10-double**

...

N-beat

A fundamental difference between this approach and traditional music theory is that the count is divided into halves instead of the entire measure. It does not matter what names are given to the notes so long as it is the count which is divided rather than the measure. A functional advantage to this is that odd times can be understood without the confusion of, for example, whether a supposedly 'whole' note only takes the duration of four beats or lasts for an entire measure. It also removed the difficulty arising from the attempt to determine the length of a supposedly 'half' note in a measure with an odd number of counts. Finally, this also does away with the notion of a 'dotted-note' which is commonly but confusingly defined as one and a half of the note's normal duration. Instead, the dotted-note concept is simply understood as three beats of whichever particular type. For those who are already familiar with the standard theory of music, here is a suggested rough translation that assumes quarter-notes are equivalent to the count-beats:

Notes	=	Beats
whole	=	bar
dotted-half	=	3-count
half	=	pulse
dotted-quarter	=	3-double
quarter	=	count
dotted-1/8th	=	3-quad
1/8th	=	double
dotted-1/16th	=	3-octo
1/16th	=	quad
dotted-1/32nd	=	3-double-octo
1/32nd	=	octo
dotted-1/64th	=	3-quad-octo
1/64th	=	double-octo
dotted-1/128th	=	3-octo-octo
1/128th	=	quad-octo
1/256th	=	octo-octo

In this practical approach to music, memorizing all these different types of note durations is absolutely unnecessary for understanding, writing, or performing music. The names presented here are merely theoretical substitutions for note names that are provided by standard music theory. Instead of using a different symbol or notational device for each one of these, I propose writing out the numbers necessary for counting, and circling the numbers that make up the desired note durations. Whenever finer divisions of the count are required, additional markings can be placed between the numbers. The numbering can be placed either below or above the corresponding notes on the musical staff. Because this approach to rhythmic notation is basically additive, the rests are already assumed, unless numbers have been circled. This makes the additional symbols for rests of different durations found in standard music theory completely superfluous.

Although more advanced rhythms are possible in music and are within the capacity of this new theory of music, they are not fundamental and therefore do not fit within the scope of this introduction. However, it might be useful to address some of the additional basic parameters that relate directly to rhythm, such as *tempo* and *dynamics*.

The tempo of a rhythm can be rigidly fixed, roughly approximate, purposefully and/or temporarily changing, indeterminately fluctuating, or even non-existent. A precise method for specifying a tempo is to list the bpm (such as 60 bpm), or even a range (such as 60-65 bpm). To allow the freedom for more interpretation, a phrase could be used to describe the tempo and feel (*however, I strongly suggest that any such phrase be written in English so as to ensure that it could be read by a large majority of people in the world without debilitating those who are already accustomed to the Italian that is traditionally used in standard music theory*). A temporary change in tempo is a *tempo modulation* and can be accomplished in a variety of ways. Here are some possible ways to notate tempo modulations:

Tempo Increase	'Speed-Up'
Slight	'T+'
Natural	'T++'
Extreme	'T+++'

Tempo Decrease	'Slow-Down'
Slight	'T-'
Natural	'T--'
Extreme	'T---'

To indicate when a tempo change is supposed to occur, as well as its duration, the tempo modulation can be connected to a range of bars or notes.

In addition to having a timing and duration, musical notes also have dynamics. A rudimentary dynamic function is the *accent* (which can be notated by a '_' underneath the count). An accent is simply an emphasized note which is typically accomplished by producing it noticeably louder than the average volume of the surrounding notes.

Connected with the accent, another basic element of dynamics is the level of loudness and intensity affecting the average volume of an entire collection of notes. This can range from extremely soft to extremely loud. With regards to loudness, here is a list of dynamic spectrum (including two additional possibilities for greater dynamic specificity) and possible ways to notate them:

1	As soft as possible	'SSS'
2	Very soft	'SS'
3	Soft	'S'
	Slightly soft	*'MS'*
4	Medium	'M'
	Slightly loud	*'ML'*
5	Loud	'L'
6	Very loud	'LL'
7	As loud as possible	'LLL'

Another element of dynamics involves modulation from one volume level to another. This can have a specific duration and intensity. As an example, a change in dynamics from as soft as possible to as loud as possible can easily be indicated by 'SSS-LLL'. The dash could also be replaced by the non-specific but commonly used '<' when going from softer to louder or '>' when going from louder to softer. To indicate the timing and duration of a dynamic modulation, this symbol can be used in relation to a range of bars or notes.

APPLICATIONS

EXPLORATION

At this point, all the basic principles and general guidelines for an introduction to music have been presented according to this new theory. The musical elements covered here include everything that is essential for beginning to explore music. But in fact, the only way to truly understand music theory is to explore it with a musical instrument for oneself. Music theory is a way to relate to music on an intellectual level, but it takes more than just knowing the theory to put it into practise, understand it, or even create it. A musical instrument gives one the means to relate to music in a practical way through hands-on experience. Practising an instrument makes it easier to relate practically to music; especially through the use of good technique. Technique helps one to relate to an instrument. It is extremely useful to seek guidance from a teacher to acquire the technique necessary for developing a working relationship with an instrument. As the relationship with an instrument develops, so does the ability to experiment with music theory and put it into practise. Finally, creativity can be thought of as a way to relate to music on an emotional level. This idea can be supported by the example of the passionate predisposition of the true artist who, driven by the creative impulse, must work out of necessity or in response to a calling. Discovering, experimenting with, and exploring music for oneself puts one in contact with the same creativity which is at the very source of music. It takes a certain creativity to find one's own ways of translating theoretical elements of music into practise rather than relying on recreational examples devised by others or blindly following specific rules. Musical exploration helps one to relate to music theoretically, practically, and creatively.

It is not the aim of this work to provide the means for putting this music theory into practise. I hope to write about the practical applications of this theory for specific instruments sometime in the future. Meanwhile, custom-tailored versions of such applications are currently limited to the talks that I have given for individuals and small groups who are interested in pursuing these ideas.

To begin exploring this theory, it is first necessary to relate the basic material to one's musical instrument. For example: If twelve notes exist, where are those notes to be found on that particular instrument? How many octaves of notes does the instrument have? If there are seven notes in a key, how is that scale pattern organized on the instrument? If there are twelve different keys, does the scale pattern look the same or different from key to key on the instrument? If there are three notes in a basic chord and two types of chords, where are the notes in relation to one another on the instrument? If there are six chords in a key, where are the notes for each chord in the scale pattern as it is organized on the instrument? Can the instrument produce multiple notes at the same time? If so, is the scale pattern arranged such that it can form full or at least partial chords? If so, what patterns can be found to form the two different types of chords? And so on.

To begin exploring rhythm, it might be useful to start by counting different examples out loud and clapping along with a metronome before applying those rhythms to an instrument. Each measure or example can be repeated indefinitely until one gets the feel of it. One could play a single note, a note combination, or a sequence of notes on an instrument to take the place of clapping. Afterwards, original rhythmic examples, patterns, and variations can be used. In devising and learning new patterns for oneself, one is simply embarking in a further exploration of music.

Once this sort of exploration has been undertaken, original notes, chords, and rhythms can be assembled according to one's own style. Similar to the way that a child plays and learns, it is not necessary to have certain parameters or particular rules in order to play with music. Besides the opportunity to engage in childlike play and to develop one's own style, one of the great aspects of musical exploration is that many of the advanced aspects of music theory can be naturally encountered and picked up along the way.

NOTATION

The most common and practical means for precisely recording music and musical ideas is in the written form of musical notation. Unfortunately, the most common system for notation which has developed alongside the standard theory of music is extremely and profoundly impractical for reasons which have been explained throughout this work. To summarize, standard notation is based upon a single key, and therefore, results in superfluous note names and additional symbols used to indicate all the notes of the chromatic scale; unique sets of additional symbols for each key; apparently different scale patterns that have different starting points for the beginning of each scale; and no visible distinctions among the natural polarities of chords within a key. In addition to these problems, there is the exclusive use of the Italian language for musical terms (at a time when the vast majority of the world uses Spanish, English, or even Mandarin Chinese), the profusion of additional symbols for potentially awkward divisions of measures; and the necessity to specify not only the durations of notes, but also of silences. Furthermore, this does not even take into consideration the many ethnomusicological and experimental difficulties which arise when attempting to notate exotic scales and tunings.

The new musical notation proposed here is the current form of a slowly evolving attempt to develop an accessible, practical means for reading and writing music. Its design was entirely derived from the foundational principles of this theory of music. It provides a universal template for all twelve keys, an ordered and recognizable layout based on the scale pattern of seven notes in a key, easy access to notes outside of the key (making all twelve notes that exist equally accessible), a consistent representation of multiple octaves, an accurate picture of the relationships between the three notes in a chord, and an intuitive way to write out rhythm that actually corresponds to the way rhythm is counted.

The new notation comfortably fits three staves on a page and three octaves onto a single staff (which was described in a previous section). The octaves can be numbered according to 'scientific music notation' in a way that best suits the range of a particular instrument. As with standard notation, additional horizontal lines can be drawn in to access additional octaves and vertical lines can be used as separators between each bar. Double vertical lines connected by an arching bracket can be used to indicate repeating bars and a number can indicate the total number of times the measures are repeated. Triple vertical lines connected by double arching brackets can be used to indicate nested repeats. A key needs to be specified prior to the actual notation; it can be represented either by the simplified note name or by note colour. Depending on the preference of the composer or the ease of use, key modulations can either be specified or based on the original key. Dots can be placed on the spaces of the staff to represent notes within the key. Dots can also be placed on the thin lines of the staff to represent notes outside the key. Diagonal lines can be used to connect notes of large intervals exceeding an octave. The tempo can be indicated next to the key and is assumed to be the dyadic pulse unless specified otherwise, depending on the composer's preference or ease of use. The count is written out so there is no need for a time signature. The counts are circled to indicate the timing and duration of the notes. The beginning of a circle must always line up with a note on the staff. The circle can extend indefinitely to include whatever duration is required. Finer divisions of time can be indicated by markers between the numbers. For example: A dot between the numbers can represent a double-count, or an 'x' surrounded by dots on either side between the numbers can represent a quad-count. There are other devices for notating more advanced rhythms as well. If multiple concurrent rhythms need to be indicated, then the numbers can be positioned next to their corresponding notes on the staff. To write out chord progressions, either the chord numbers can be written on top of the staff or the chord note can be marked on the staff and circled.

The notation introduced here is not in any complete or final form. It is constantly being added to, improved, and revised. Hopefully, this ongoing work will result in a very accessible and practical means for recording music in a written form that is adaptable enough to keep up with the evolution of the very musical composers and performers that music notation is meant to serve.

POSSIBILITIES

There are other fully and partially developed parts of this music theory which are not included because they are more advanced and require some kind of fundamental understanding of music. Currently, entire chapters could be devoted to each of the numbers 1-9 (along with others) and their relationships to various aspects of music. As a foretaste for those who already have an understanding of music, some of the items yet to be covered include: harmonics, temperaments, intervals, intervallic movement, chordal movement, complex chords, harmony, modulation, key regions, modality, pentatonic scales, hexatonic scales (including the whole-tone and augmented scales), alternative heptatonic scales (including the harmonic and melodic minor scales), octotonic scales (including bebop scales), enneatonic scales, exotic pentatonic scales (as in Japanese and Indian music), exotic heptatonic scales (as in Arabic and Indian music), dodecaphonic systems, shuffle and swing rhythms, tuplets, polymetres, polyrhythms, and more. All of these aspects of music are well within the capacity of this theory of music and new notation. This system has the potential to adapt very well to the exotic scales and tunings that are studied by ethnomusicologists but consistently fail to translate practically into the existing theory and notation. It can also serve to address the more experimental concerns of contemporary composers and music theorists. Most importantly, it makes the language of music more accessible to people who seek to become an instrument for the creative impulse.

One of the concerns that might be expressed in response to this theory of music is that it is initially founded upon the notion of 'equal temperament'. Many questions have been raised about the effectiveness of equally distributing the tunings of notes in the chromatic scale because equal temperament disturbs the natural harmonic properties of the notes. It is my opinion that equal temperament is the perfect balance between a theoretical ideal and a practical compromise. However, it is also my opinion that other temperaments and systems of tuning are extremely important aspects of music theory which are able to provide a technically advanced dimension of subtlety. In fact, it is only with regards to temperament that I personally have any remaining appreciation for the traditional system of notation. This is due to the fact that the additional note names and symbols at one time indicated subtle differences in the tunings of sharps, flats, and naturals for instruments on which small adjustments in tuning are possible. The construction of many instruments does not easily allow for such slight manipulations of the notes to be made during performance, which makes such fine-tuning impractical as a universal approach. Regardless of the temperament, the basic operation of the notes remains same. Equal temperament is the most practical option and therefore ought to be the standard for introducing music theory. Achieving the nuances of other temperaments is something aspiring musicians should probably explore once they are ready to learn the more advanced elements of music. Along with the issues of various temperaments, exotic tunings and differing numbers of chromatic divisions should be considered as special elements of music. Most commonly, these bear some kind of relationship to the twelve notes of the chromatic scale. For example, the ancient Chinese gamut is based on twelve notes which, in turn, yield twelve different subsets of twelve notes. Another example is Indian music, which contains twenty-two *shrutis* (unequal chromatic divisions). From these shrutis are selected the tunings for the twelve *swaras* (notes of an Indian chromatic scale) from which seven notes are selected to create a *thaat* (a scale in Hindustani music) or *mela* (a scale in Karnatak music). Although there are examples of chromatic equivalents based on numbers other than twelve, they are relatively uncommon and should be understood as special cases with regards to the fundamental principles of music theory.

Another issue some may have with this theory is that the original scale used here is made up of seven notes (a *heptatonic* scale). The reason for such a dispute may be that five-note scales (or *pentatonic* scales) are also found throughout the world and throughout history. More significantly, the earliest examples we have of musical instruments appear to be based on pentatonic scales. However, historical evidence of the heptatonic scale has been found carved onto an ancient Babylonian stone tablet known as CBS 1766, dating around 1500 BC. In his essay 'Earliest Evidence of Heptatonism', Richard J. Dumbrill interpreted this carving as a documentation of heptatonic scales. Along with the cuneiform writing on the tablet, there is a diagram of a heptagram within two concentric circles. This diagram bears a striking resemblance to a heptagram that can be constructed by connecting each of the notes arranged in a circle to notes either four or five scale-degrees apart. Once all the notes are connected in this way, a very similar seven-pointed star is formed; this star is primarily based upon the intervals of the fourth and fifth. In addition to this example, a tuning text for a heptatonic scale was found on tablet UET VII 74, dating around 1800 BC, and an early text on musical notation that referenced two octaves of a heptatonic scale was found on tablet MS 5105, dating somewhere between 2000 and 1600 BC.

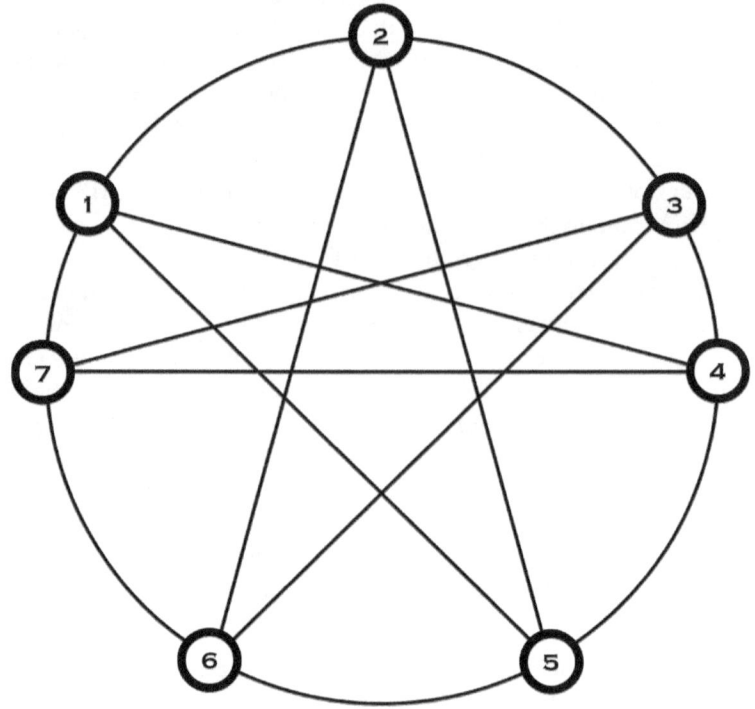

In addition, the most ancient instruments found are typically wind instruments that are capable of bending notes to fill in the large gaps of a pentatonic scale. Note-bending musical ornamentations provide access to the notes of a heptatonic scale which are missing from the pentatonic. The basic pentatonic scale contains the most harmonious notes and intervals found within the basic heptatonic scale. Therefore, it would make sense for ancient musical instrument makers to initially focus on constructing a device for producing the five most harmonious notes, leaving it to the technique of musicians to produce any of the other notes.

This new theory of music has the potential to bring the understanding of music closer to those who have a real interest by simplifying and ordering all the different elements of music into a coherent whole and then relating this whole in a way that is both definitive and comprehensive. By exploring the theory for oneself rather than through historical examples, aspiring musicians can creatively acquire musical knowledge without compromising their individual originality. At the same time, this theory can also be used as a tool to bring into reach the various musical traditions throughout the world and throughout history. This theory has the potential to be used with any musical instrument, style, or setting. The possibilities opened up by the new notation include an intuitive and practical means of recording music, a means for making historical works more versatile and accessible, and a framework that is adaptable to exotic and experimental musics.

References

The following is a general list of references used up to this point in the ongoing development of this new theory of music. Each work referenced should be taken in its entirety rather than in specific extracted portions, so as to comprehend the integrity of the collection of ideas it conveys or represents. To disregard the context of a particular part of one of these works places one at risk of missing that which was truly referenced. On the other hand, if there are any shortcoming within this book in how the referenced material was understood or applied, the fault is likely to be my own rather than that of the referenced authors. I do not claim to represent the intentions of the authors, but merely to work from my own understanding of their works.

This list is by no means comprehensive or complete; it is merely a growing collection of works that are essential for understanding the building blocks of this theory. In addition to the following referenced materials, there are many individuals who have made themselves available to me as I have developed this work. There are also hundreds of minor references that I have used along the way that I have either overlooked or left unrecorded. I mention this in advance as an apology for any missing or forgotten information that I might have failed to include here.

Finally, if many of the references appear to be unrelated to music, it is because most of the ideas for this approach to music have stemmed from my own search for the esoteric teachings of Christianity. Initially, I began writing a book about Christianity and later shelved it to write about music. Once I began writing about music, it turned out that I was also writing a book that indirectly corresponds to Christianity. It is on this note that the book will end, in the same way that it began: Music is mysterious.

Ashton, Anthony. *Harmonograph: A Visual Guide to the Mathematics of Music.* New York: Walker, 2003.

Austin, James H. *Zen and the Brain: Toward an Understanding of Meditation and Consciousness.* Cambridge: MIT Press, 1925.

Bennett, J. G. *Making a Soul: Human Destiny and the Debt of Our Existence.* Santa Fe: Bennett Books, 1954.

Bennett, J. G. *The Dramatic Universe.* Vol 1, *The Foundations of Natural Philosophy.* Santa Fe: Bennett Books, 1956.

Bennett, J. G. *The Dramatic Universe.* Vol 2, *The Foundations of Moral Philosophy.* Santa Fe: Bennett Books, 1961.

Bennett, J. G. *Elementary Systematics: A Tool for Understanding Wholes.* Santa Fe: Bennett Books, 1963.

Bennett, J. G. *Creative Thinking.* Santa Fe: Bennett Books, 1964.

Bennett, J. G. *A Spiritual Psychology.* Lakemont, GA: CSA Press, 1964.

Bennett, J. G. *The Dramatic Universe.* Vol 3, *Man and His Nature.* Santa Fe: Bennett Books, 1966.

Bennett, J. G. *The Dramatic Universe.* Vol 4, *History.* Santa Fe: Bennett Books, 1966.

Bennett, J. G. 'Talks and Lectures: 1971-1974.' Lecture, Sherborne Acadamy, December 11, 1974. The Estate of J. G. Bennett, England.

Bennett, J. G. *Transformation.* Charles Town, WV: Claymont Communications, 1978.

Bennett, J. G.. *Deeper Man.* London: Turnstone Books, 1978.

Bennett, John G. *Energies: Material, Vital, Cosmic.* Charles Town, WV: Claymont Communications, 1964.

Bennett, John G., and A. G. E. Blake. *Existence*. Sherborne, Glos.: Coombe Springs Press, 1977.

Bennett, John G. *The Sevenfold Work*. Charles Town, WV: Claymont Communications, 1979.

Bennett, John G. *Enneagram Studies,* rev. ed. York Beach, ME: S. Weiser, 1983.

Bennett, John G. *The Way To Be Free*. 1980. Reprint, New York: Weiser, 1992.

Bennett, John G., and A. G. E. Blake. *Creation,* lst Bennett Book ed. Santa Fe: Bennett Books, 1998.

Bennett, John G. *The First Liberation: Working with Themes at Sherborne House*. Santa Fe: Bennett Books, 2002.

Benton, Janetta Rebold, and Robert DiYanni. *Arts and Culture: An Introduction to the Humanities*. New York: Custom Publishing, 2008.

Black Belt Guitar Academy. 'Black Belt Guitar Academy.' www.blackbeltguitar.com (accessed October 5, 2012).

Blumberg, Roger E. 'TheCipher.com_Home: Blumberg's Music Theory Cipher for Guitar and Mandolin.' http://www.thecipher.com (accessed October 5, 2012).

Bullinger, E. W. *Number in Scripture: Its Supernatural Design and Spiritual Significance*. Grand Rapids: Kregel Publications, 1967.

Capuzzo, Guy. 'Pat Martino's The Nature of the Guitar: An Intersection of Jazz Theory and Neo-Riemannian Theory.' *The Online Journal of Society For Music Theory* 12, no. 1 (2006).

http://www.mtosmt.org/issues/mto.06.12.1/mto.06.12.1.capuzzo.
pdf (accessed October 5, 2012).

Conze, Edward. *Buddhist Scriptures.* Harmondsworth, Middlesex, UK:
Penguin Books, 1959.

Cymatics Soundscapes . VHS. Directed by Hans Jenny. Newmarket, NH:
Macromedia Publishing, 1980.

Dumbrill, Richard. 'The Earliest Evidence of Heptatonism in a Late Old
Babylonian Text: CBS 1766.' Academia.edu.
http://www.academia.edu/243915/Earliest_Evidence_of_Heptat
onism (accessed October 29, 2012).

Evans, Roger. *How To Read Music: The Fundamentals of Music Notation
Made Easy.* New York: Crown Trade Paperbacks, 1978.

Fripp, Robert. 'DGM Live!' http://www.dgmlive.com (accessed March 26,
2011).

Fripp, Robert. 'Guitar Craft.' http://www.guitarcraft.com (accessed March
26, 2011).

Fripp, Robert. 'From Good To Great: Beginner to Mastery.' Keynote
speech, National Speakers Association SpeakerPalooza - Patricia
Fripp, February 1, 2008.

Fripp, Robert. 'Unplugged.' Addresses From Many Events - Patricia Fripp,
1997-1998.

Goddard, Dwight. *A Buddhist Bible.* 1938. Reprint, Boston: Beacon Press,
1970.

Godwin, Joscelyn. *Music, Mysticism, and Magic: A Sourcebook.* London:
Routledge & Kegan Paul, 1986.

Gold, Jude. 'Sacred Geometry: Simplifying the Fretboard with Pat Martino.' *Guitar Player*, April 1, 2004. http://www.patmartino.com/Articles/GuitarPlayer_April_2004.pdf (accessed October 5, 2012).

Goodall, Dominic. *Hindu Scriptures*. London: Phoenix Press, 1996.

Gurdjieff, G. I. *Views From The Real World*. New York: Penguin Compass, 1973.

Gurdjieff, G. I. *Life Is Real Only Then, When 'I Am'*. 1975. Reprint, London: Arkana Penguin Books, 1991.

Gurdjieff, G. I. *Beelzebub's Tales To His Grandson: An Objectively Impartial Criticism of the Life of Man*. 1950. Reprint, New York: Arkana Penguin, 1999.

Gurdjieff, G. I. *Transcripts Of Gurdjieff's Meetings 1941-1946*. London: Book Studio, 2009.

Gurdjieff, Georges Ivanovitch. *Meetings With Remarkable Men*. New York: E. P. Dutton, 1969.

Haleem, M. A. *The Qur'an*. New York: Oxford University Press, 2005.

Helmholtz, Hermann L. F. *On the Sensations of Tone: As a Physiological Basis   for the Theory of Music*, 2nd ed. New York: Dover Publications,   1954.

Helminski, Kabir Edmund. *Living Presence: A Sufi Way to Mindfulness and the Essential Self*. New York: Penguin Putnam, 1992.

Iazzetti, Giovanni, and Enrico Rigutti. *Atlas of Human Anatomy*. 2007. Reprint, Cobham, Surrey: Taj Books, Ltd., 2002.

Kadmon, Adam. *The Guitar Grimoire: A Compendium of Formulas for Guitar Scales and Modes.* New York: produced by Metatron Inc. for Carl Fischer, 1995.

Kaplan, Aryeh. *Sefer Yetzirah (The Book of Creation): In Theory and Practice.* 1997, rev. ed. York Beach, ME: S. Weiser, 1990.

Kuchinsky, Saul, and John G. Bennett. *Systematics: Search for Miraculous Management.* Charles Town, WV: Claymont Communications, 1985.

Lateef, Yusef. *Repository Of Scales And Melodic Patterns.* Amherst, MA: Fana Music, 1981.

Lau, D. C. *Lao Tzu: Tao Te Ching.* New York: Penguin Books, 1963.

Lee, H. D. P. *Timaeus and Critias.* Harmondsworth, UK: Penguin Books, 1971.

Le Mee, Katharine W. *Chant: The Origins, Form, Practice, and Healing Power of Gregorian Chant.* New York: Bell Tower, 1994.

Liu, Yiming, Boduan Zhang, and Thomas F. Cleary. *The Inner Teachings Of Taoism.* Boston: Shambhala, 1986.

Lucy, Charles E. H. 'LucyTuning*LucyScaleDevelopments*LucyTuned Lullabies*Pi tuning*John Longitude Harrison.' http://www.lucytune.com (accessed October 5, 2012).

Lundy, Miranda. *Sacred Number: The Secret Qualities of Quantities.* New York: Walker & Co., 2005.

Mascaro, Juan. *The Dhammapada: The Path of Perfection.* Harmondsworth, UK: Penguin Books, 1973.

May, Elizabeth. *Musics Of Many Cultures: An Introduction*. Berkeley: University of California Press, 1980.

Meetings With Remarkable Men. VHS. Directed by Peter Brook. New York: Parabola, 1979.

Merton, Thomas. *Contemplative Prayer*. New York: Herder and Herder, 1969.

Milne, Andrew. 'The Tonal Centre: Tonality.' http://www.tonalcentre.org (accessed October 5, 2012).

Mlely, G. F. *The 8-Tone Quarto-Modes Concept*. Long Beach, CA: JazCraft, 2010.

New American Standard Bible. Anaheim: Foundation Publications, publisher for the Lockman Foundation, 1997.

Nicoll, Maurice. *Psychological Commentaries Six-Volume Set: On the Teaching of Gurdjieff & Ouspensky*. York Beach, ME: Samuel Weiser, 1996.

Ocvirk, Otto G. *Art Fundamentals: Theory and Practice*, 2nd ed. Dubuque, IA: W.C. Brown Co., 1968.

Oke, Vidyadhar. '22 Shruti Harmonium Homepage.' 22 Shruti. www.22shruti.com (accessed October 5, 2012).

Olivelle, Patrick. *Upanisads*. Oxford: Oxford Univ. Press, 1998.

Ouspensky, P. D. *The Fourth Way: An Arrangement by Subject of Verbatim Extracts from the Records of Ouspensky's Meetings in London and New York, 1921-1946*. 1957. Reprint, New York: Vintage Books, 1971.

Ouspensky, P. D. *The Psychology Of Man's Possible Evolution*. 1950. Reprint, New York: Vintage Books, 1974.

Ouspensky, P. D. *A Further Record: Extracts from Meetings 1928-1945*. 1986. Reprint, London and New York: Arkana Paperbacks, 1987.

Ouspensky, P. D. *A Record of Meetings*. 1951. Reprint, New York: Arkana Penguin, 1992.

Ouspensky, P. D. *In Search of The Miraculous: Fragments of an Unknown Teaching*. San Diego: Harcourt, 2001.

Pi. DVD. Directed by Darren Aronofsky. Chicago: Lions Gate, 1998.

Powers, Cameron. *Arabic Musical Scales: Basic Maqam Teachings*. Boulder, CO: G. L. Design, 2005.

Sachs, Curt. *The Rise Of Music In The Ancient World, East and West*. New York: W. W. Norton & Co., 1943.

Sayre, Henry M. *A World Of Art*, 2nd ed. Upper Saddle River, NJ: Prentice Hall, 1997.

Schoenberg, Arnold, and Leonard Stein. *Structural Functions Of Harmony*, rev. ed. New York: W. W. Norton, 1969.

Schoenberg, Arnold. *Theory of Harmony*, 3rd ed. Berkley and Los Angeles: University of California Press, 1978.

Sekida, Kazuki. *Zen Training: Methods and Philosophy*. New York: Weatherhill, 1975.

Slonimsky, Nicolas. *Thesaurus Of Scales and Melodic Patterns*. New York: Scribner's, 1947.

Speeth, Kathleen Riordan. *The Gurdjieff Work*. New York: Penguin Putnam Inc., 1989.

Tanakh, The Holy Scriptures: The New JPS Translation According to the Traditional Hebrew Text. Philadelphia: Jewish Publication Society, 1985.

Titon, Jeff Todd. *Worlds Of Music: An Introduction to the Music of the World's Peoples*. New York: Schirmer Books, 1984.

Touch the Sound. DVD. Directed by Thomas Riedelsheimer. Waterville: Shadow Distribution, 2004.

Waking Life. DVD. Directed by Richard Linklater. Los Angeles: Fox Searchlight Pictures, 2001.

Waldberg, Michel. *Gurdjieff: An Approach to His Ideas*. London: Routledge & Kegan Paul Ltd, 1981.

Wilhelm, Hellmut, and Richard Wilhelm. *Understanding the I Ching: The Wilhelm Lectures on the Book of Changes*. Princeton: Princeton University Press, 1995.

Wilhelm, Richard. *I Ching: Book of Changes*. Hoo, Kent: Grange Books, 2001.

Yamaguchi, Masaya. *Pentatonicism In Jazz: Creative Aspects and Practice*, rev. ed. New York: Masaya Music Services, 2006.

Zeilik, Michael. *Astronomy: The Evolving Universe*, 9th ed. Cambridge, UK: Cambridge University Press, 2002.